Dearest Larry,

Welcome Home !

I hope your trip was fantastic !

We are kindred women in many, many ways.

May this book help you to Arise [...] important

In love. C.C.

Arise, Beloved

Trilogy Christian Publishers
A Wholly Owned Subsidiary of Trinity Broadcasting Network
2442 Michelle Drive | Tustin, CA 92780

For information, address Trilogy Christian Publishing
Rights Department, 2442 Michelle Drive, Tustin, Ca 92780.
Trilogy Christian Publishing/ TBN and colophon are trademarks of Trinity Broadcasting Network.

For information about special discounts for bulk purchases, please contact Trilogy Christian Publishing.

Manufactured in the United States of America
10 9 8 7 6 5 4 3 2 1
Library of Congress Cataloging-in-Publication Data is available.
ISBN 978-1-64088-083-2
ISBN 978-1-64088-084-9 (ebook)

C.C. EVANS-PUGLISE

Arise, Beloved

HOW ORDINARY WOMEN AWAKEN

TO *Extraordinary* LIVES

THE ONLY THING WORSE
THAN BEING BLIND IS
having sight
BUT NO *vision*

-HELEN KELLER

I am not Helen Keller.

My sight has dipped slightly with the onset of early middle age, but I see well and all around. My hearing is sound as ever, but much of my life I have felt blind and deaf. Missing critical signals and warnings. Failing to hear or respond to life like I needed to. Fumbling around in the dark instead. Bumping into painful reminders that things needed to change. Waiting for someone else to come and create the changes I yearned for. Blind and deaf to the knowledge that many of the changes needed to be authored by me.

I should have awakened many times before I did. Certainly, by forty, I should have had many of these truths under my belt:

- **PEOPLE YOU LOVE LEAVE. LOVE DOESN'T GUARANTEE US ANYTHING.**

- DEATH COMES FOR ALL OF US, EVEN THE YOUNG.

- FAITH DOESN'T PROTECT YOU FROM HEART-BREAK AND NEITHER DOES EDUCATION. (EVEN IF YOU HAVE LOTS OF BOTH.)

I should have learned, at least before forty, these basic essentials:

- YOU CAN'T AND PROBABLY WON'T CHANGE PEOPLE. (EVEN IF YOU REALLY LOVE THEM, AND THE CHANGE MIGHT BE BEST FOR THEM.)

- MUCH OF WHAT YOU ADMIRE IN OTHERS IS SOMETHING YOU TOO COULD BE DOING BUT ARE NOT — YET.

- REGRETS OF OLD OFTEN REAR UP IN YOUR LIFE DISGUISED WITH DIFFERENT FACES OF MAKEUP.

- REPAIR OFTEN COMES FROM DOING NOW WHAT WE WISH WE WOULD HAVE DONE THEN.

- LIFE IS BETTER WHEN YOU ARE CHASING DREAMS INSTEAD OF APPROVAL.

- SELF-PREOCCUPATION IS BONDAGE — AND SO IS THE PERCEPTION OF WHAT OTHERS THINK OF US.

- WHAT WE THINK ABOUT OURSELVES USUALLY DETERMINES OUR LIFE, OUR COURSE, AND OUR CAPACITY.

- SOMETIMES, EVEN IN OUR MOST ESSENTIAL AND FORMATIVE RELATIONSHIPS, WE DON'T GET THE RESOLUTION WE CRAVE. SOMETIMES WE NEVER GET A REDO, EDIT, OR CAN GO BACK TO THE START TO MAKE A RELATIONSHIP BETTER; SO, WE LEARN TO TRUST GOD INSTEAD.

Perhaps we have much in common. Perhaps you have been awakened by degrees. Perhaps you too have been nudged into awareness during the course of your life, gently rocking you awake. You are sitting in a place now with eyes partially or wide open.

You are in the dark until one day you are not. You

are sleeping until one day you are awake. You are blind and deaf until, one day, you see and you hear. One day, you are awakened by vision, and your life will never be the same.

May I invite you into this adventure, this journey of awakening and authenticating your own life, becoming the woman you crave to be; this life of love, joy, and wild personal freedom you were designed to live? Oh good, beloved, I will be holding your hand on each shared step of this journey. Destiny awaits us both, my friend.

Our journey will always be richer, deeper, and more earnest when paper and pen meet. Would you choose a tablet, a legal pad, or a journal you are willing to take on this journey? Would you give yourself the time and the space to write and describe where your mind and heart take you while and after you work with each chapter? Will you create a mental and physical space and discipline yourself to respond in writing to your stirrings, your own precious insight and wisdom? May you own your journey by adding your signature responses at the end of each chapter. I conclude every chapter with Practical and Spiritual Steps to help you dive deeper into the content, claiming each step as your own.

Life and love and victory abound when we awaken to awareness of our lives. And to celebrate awakening, a French Press moment is included in every chapter. In these moments, we lift our mugs of coffee, of lemon water or tea, and celebrate the little victories we learn to make happen, that change our lives.

Dedicated to my A-team

I had a lovely friend describe her A-team to me. I could understand every public figure, why she chose them, what they offer her life. But when I think of my own, I think about the people I live life with. The ones who call me higher everyday of my life, the ones who call me to lean into my dreams, to work and write from the bone. The people who remind me to do everything with excellence, even if it means, starting over.

Thank you: Alice Nowakowski, Katrina Munoz, Donna Vail and Gwyn Erwin, my midwives for this book, and for the countless other miracles that your lives offer, in daily ways, to mine. You raise the bar, you break the mold, you are gifts from God. This book would never have been written without your heart and soul investment in me.

I thank you Sarah Rasmussen for your poetic muse in my life, for your dedication and leadership in brainstorming this title.

Amanda Stuart for convincing me that if I could dream it, I could do it.

Lina Benbrook for your loyal and steadfast support of me, for watching my kids, for free, so I could write, or just sit still and breathe. For the countless times you told me you heard the heart of God in my writing, and asking me to continue when I only felt defeat. Thank you.

April and Kevin Pitts for reminding me why the cover needed to have dandelions and the hope they call us to. I thank you both for decades of friendship that has not failed.

I thank you Joseph Puglise, my husband, who knew this book was in me over a decade before I did. Thank you for calling me to discipline and hard and excellent work. Your faith in me has been enormous, and is, indeed, part of the reason this book is complete.

How can I ever say thank you to the women who help me raise my girls, and keep my home place of joy, inspiration and belonging? I say thank you to Rebecca Dominquez, Erica Vazquez, Mariana Contreras and Terry Illiano. You are family to me and always will be.

I thank my godparents and pastors, Bob and Penny Fulton, for your decades of faithful and nourishing instruction over my life. I know miracles are possible because of your teachings. I believe in them.

I see them in your lives of legacy. Thank you prophet Carl for your submitted heart, for your words of knowledge and prophecy, I have sightings of them sprouting and growing all over my life. You shifted my life into freedom.

I thank you, Jeanette Rodriguez, for the elegance and excellence you bring to this book. For making my words come alive in technicolor. Thank you for your countless revisions to bring my thoughts to life. I am ever grateful for you.

To Daja who makes our family, our lives, our possibilities, our hopes and dreams, attainable, thank you. You are loved beyond words.

Last but not least, I thank my Facebook group, Women of Legacy, who have called me to higher ground since its inception May, 2017. I wake up grateful each morning because of you, and you have called me into consistency, and into an inspiration I have never known until we met, and gathered 3 days a week.

My cup, overflows. Truly.

C.C. Evans-Puglise
CCEvansPuglise.com

Table of Contents

A KIND OF LIGHT SPREAD OUT FROM HER.

AND EVERYTHING CHANGED COLOR.

AND THE WORLD OPENED OUT.

AND A DAY WAS GOOD TO AWAKEN TO.

AND THERE WERE NO LIMITS TO ANYTHING.

AND THE PEOPLE OF THE WORLD
WERE GOOD AND HANDSOME.

*And I was not
afraid anymore.*

-JOHN STEINBECK

CHAPTER 1

Awakening

Bits and pieces and fragments of life are waking us up all the time. I am confident I have never laid my head down any night as the same woman. Subtle change is constantly moving me, reshaping me, groggily stumbling me out of bed, dragging me out of slumber. Life is always sending me alarms to prompt consciousness, serving me cups of coffee to open my eyes, commanding them to get fixed and focused on my life.

I was awakened to deep and uncontrollable grief before I was awakened to anything else. The first time I remember life awakening me like this, I was eleven years old, self-centered, preoccupied with Jordache jeans and Michael Jackson, wanting to wear makeup and shave my legs.

My seventh-grade day ended with a standing 3:30 phone call with my best friend Christina, who went to school on the other side of town. I was unprepared to hear Christina's mother answer the phone in a tone

I could not name or comprehend. In an ominous tone that did not change, she abruptly instructed me to have my mom phone her when she got home. Irritated, I asked why, only to hear a dial tone.

I waited on our porch for what felt like the rest of spring for my mom to push those fateful seven numbers that would change the entire course of my life. With a face whiter than a Colorado winter snow, my mom repeated the words, "I'm sorry," so many times that my body began to rock with each one uttered. My mom held me with eyes that I could not read or understand while time and blood flow stopped for us both.

Earlier that day, Christina had jumped off a high-rise building downtown, while I was learning the states and capitals in Mr. Regan's history class. There was no note, no explanation; only the introduction to a bone-chilling grief that can happen when you are awakened to knowing that death comes even for the very young. Death comes before you are prepared or ready or can say goodbye. Death comes.

I did not know then the impact Christina's death would have on me. I did not know that twenty years later, I would spend eleven years in graduate school to become a psychoanalyst to help find words for unbearable states of my mind. I did not know her death would influence me to put words to our private, secret struggles so we wouldn't suffer in isolation. I did not know it would invite me into a life path where I would choose to be as honest about the personal pain I know intimately, so others could bring their own alongside me, to meet one another in a place of earnestness, hold each other's hands while we breathe deeper into this life that death can steal.

I WAS AWAKENED TO HEARTBREAK OF THE ROMANTIC SORT WHEN I WAS IN HIGH SCHOOL.

Still very self-preoccupied, self-interested, and centered in the middle of my own thoughts and agendas, I was in love with a boy who made me believe human perfection was real, true love was entirely possible, and bliss attainable through dating. I wrote love letters and poems and sprayed them with perfume. I could not sing, I cannot sing, but if I had been able to, I would have written saccharine sweet music and sung songs at top volume. Unabashedly.

I was not looking for signs to counter my sentiments. I did not pay attention to warnings that love was shifting, lessening, and leaving. When my boyfriend broke up with me for someone who was smarter and more outgoing than I, I was awakened by the knowing that reality often trumps fantasy, that people you love leave. Even if you love them with every fiber inside you, relationships still end.

These losses of love shape us, don't they? They form us, chiseling us out on the inside and furnishing perspective and a lens for our lives. My first therapist was a lovely, gentle man, who taught me how to think in relational truths in the throes of graduate school. He would craft his own story of early heartbreak into clinical words that would display how the early rupture of love found its way into his marriage and became woven into his life story — not with tragedy or morbidity, but because life and love and loss taught him the power of relational impact, the knowing that relationships never come to a neat and tidy close, a bow wrapped all around. On the heels of another breakup, he told me, "Relationships never do end. People just stop seeing each other, but the relationship still lives." I understand this to be true twenty years later. All our loves and losses carve into us, tattoo us somewhere inside, lingering and marking us.

SOME BLASPHEMOUS PLACE YOU LEARN THAT EDUCATION WILL PROTECT YOU, OUTSMART YOUR CIRCUMSTANCES FROM LOSS, AND HEDGE A RING OF PROTECTION AROUND YOU. ENCASE YOU. BUBBLE YOU UP. LIES. LIES THAT YOU CAN BELIEVE, BANK ON, CRAFT YOUR LIFE AROUND.

I did a full court press in pursuit of psychology. I took every available undergraduate course on understanding the human mind and then chased down more knowledge, more education, getting a master's in psychology and then a doctorate in psychoanalysis. I had riddles of pain in my life, so I turned toward graduate level psychology to help me solve them. I was desperate to find answers that spoke simple truths on how to stop people from hurting me, make them change their mind about me, and fight for me instead of against me.

Have you too ever wanted these answers? Have you ever hoped you could study your way out of pain? Outsmart it?

I wish it worked. I lived like it was working, until one day I awakened, knowing that nothing I had done was working at all. I had everything I had ever been chasing: I had the perfect pant size, an amazing job, a private practice, no debt, an Ivy League boyfriend. But on the inside, I was as alive as a tomb.

One day, I dissolved into the blubbery kind of bawling in the parking lot of a church, too overwhelmed by emptiness to drive, too incapacitated to get out of the car. I knew my life wasn't working, even though all the moving parts were in order, and everything on paper was checked off. I awakened to the knowing of how desperately I yearned for the peace that comes from having reconciled my heart to God. I made a divine exchange that day: my life for His life through me. I completed a very simple equation that day: I gave Him my life, and He gave me one worth living; but I did not know the work of heart that life with Him would require.

I BELIEVE IN A GOD WHO GIVES HIS PEOPLE AN ABUNDANT LIFE, FULL OF MERCY AND GOODNESS AND BEAUTY ALL AROUND. BUT WOULD YOU AGREE

THAT ABUNDANCE DOES NOT MEAN BLISS OR PERFECTION, OR THAT DARKNESS AND SADNESS WILL LIFT COMPLETELY? WE STILL HOLD GIANTS INSIDE OURSELVES. WE STILL HOLD LIVES OF PROFOUND TEXTURES. GREY AND DARK STILL REVEAL THEMSELVES, DON'T THEY?

Do you know that faith doesn't protect you from heart-break, no matter how strong it is? Heartbreak still comes, and life still breaks over and over, doesn't it?

My memory often blurs my childhood down into vague impressions, isolated pictures. I remember random details, like picking blackberries in Colorado summers, a babysitter who was often drunk and passed out but let my friend and I take turns sitting on her lap to drive. I remember going door-to-door, selling spice racks for a school fundraiser, and my mom and I driving from Colorado to California in a convertible with Elvis and Willie Nelson blaring, summer wind racing through our hair. But these feel like pictures, not tangible, something I can see but cannot touch. But losses and breakups and death I can feel. I can step back into those moments, replay conversations word for word. I can go back into those moments and give you a play by play, tell you what the air smelled like and what I was staring at as I was saying goodbye. There is something about finality and goodbyes that has always made me show up in full presence, lose my ability to drift and to daydream, and sink me into a bed of nails — restoring my consciousness like an ice bucket of water thrown on me, my teeth chattering, my body chilled to the bone. Fully awake.

I see those goodbyes as teachers now, teaching me how much of my childhood I spent chasing redemption from the yearning to be the apple of my father's eye, the hope that repair would come through a single word or deed that would right so many wrongs. I spent many of my childhood moments curled up on a tear-soaked pillow, waiting on an apology, a repair, a kiss to an injured place. All those moments would pass as naturally as seasons, and all I was waiting for never came. I tucked those injuries in a place recessed deep inside of me, then carried them into the next relationship for repair — and the next and the next — always hoping life and romance and relationships would restore what had been lost through the heartbreak that comes when your dad cannot see you, cannot hear you, and you blame the blindness and deafness on yourself.

I was a little girl broken, in part because I could not access my father. I grew into a woman who would choose men laden with the same inaccessibility, the same distance. Every goodbye alerted me to my internal blueprint for my choice of man: distant, distressing, and often drunk. Goodbyes awakened me to the knowing that repair was never going to come from the person I was saying goodbye to.

Beloved, have you learned this too? Have you been violated, stolen from, hurt, abused, and awakened to the knowing that the perpetrator can never give back to you what has been taken? We must deal with ourselves in this place of enormous loss and cry out in hope that God alone will restore. He can become our recompense in a place dark and bleak. The sobering wake-up call is that love and life can't hand us what we most ache for, and that closure and completeness often do not come from the conversations we crave.

I was forced by life to awaken to the real awakening: What I had been chasing in relationships had more to do with me than men. It held a lot less to do with what a man thought of me and a whole lot more to do with what I thought about myself. A big and mighty "aha" was the realization that the conversation I constantly pursued with men was a conversation I actually needed to have with myself. The awakening was when I recognized that all the keys I chased down in relationships outside of me, I held inside of me.

You have them too, beloved. These keys to unlock the life you crave, the one you yearn for, infinite power, are indeed accessible and inside us all. We roam through a maze in life, groping for clarity, assurance, the lit-up path. We bang our heads on locked doors, stumble down nowhere roads, get flattened by the steamrollers of life. Then one day, hope comes, and awakening shows up alongside it. We pick ourselves up from the ground, a little dusty, a little dirty, but ready to handle our lives. And no one has told us before of the rush and the energy that comes when we are done with excuses and are ready to handle our lives, to own our choices and unlock the power inside us. We realize the home we have always yearned for lives inside of us. We can rest, because the searching is over. What we have lost in life is found. We have come full circle.

I wish I could ask you where life has stunned

you. I wish I could know your losses, the areas life has punched the wind out of you. I would hold your hand while I hear your astounding story. We come alive when someone hears us on our deepest levels, don't we? When they not only hear us but understand us, get us, climb inside our inner chambers, and sit down for tea. When they are present, available, and beside us as we journey in union through our own story, discovering treasures. When we break out in shared chills because of a piece of truth we are both holding, and awe moves through every hair follicle of our arms at precisely the same speed. Connection does this, doesn't it? When we land on truth, it changes us on the inside, doesn't it? Truth creates new beings out of us, flooding us with the awareness of how much light we carry. Awakening.

Surely, love, loss, grief, and abject misery can wake us up, but there is another kind of awakening we yearn for, one encoded in our bones and soul. There is an awakening when we discover every layer of injury, every soiled and spotted story, every imagination we have ever held that disqualified us — all these can be used to whisper us into destiny. They usher us into a place where the losses knit into a tapestry of pain that is rich and textured enough to envelope another, because we know and understand pain in its wild detail and complexity. We become ready and prepared to work with our failures and our fractures, then to use our lives unabashedly. As heat and pressure in the earth birth diamonds, heat and pressure from our lives can fix us in a corner where our only option is to awaken to our truest voice, dull the deafening noise of the world around us, raise the volume of the still small voice within that smacks of truth like none we could ever hear or imagine — and calls us awake.

Stillness is this presence, causing us to hear, to know, and to feel; beckoning us to finding truth, learning the luxurious sound of our own voice. This is where we can stand in a place of immoveable knowing, the knowing that the power in our lives does not come from our circumstances, our shoe collection, the cushion in our wallet or bank account, but it comes from inside us. It is in our bellies. We can feel the truth of who we are, where we stand. All that we think and know and feel.

The mind can spin, but your knowing, your truth, your awakening, comes from your belly. Awakening comes when we listen, when we heed, when we make our decisions out of stillness rather than frenzy, and we make them from the seat of truth rather than the chatter of our minds. We become clear and immovable, because the still, small voice is stronger and has more weight and heft than any other. We can name what we need, what we want, stand in our truth, our knowing, and all the king's horses and all the king's men cannot change our mind. We are not batted around when we awaken to this voice and slow down our time and decision-making, because we are present and awake, responsive to it.

We start to surge with hope, when we know that we don't need a shopping spree, or to lose those pesky fifteen pounds, or change someone's mind about us, because we are carrying a solution far more powerful. We are the carriers of stillness. We are bearers of presence. We are holding our own ring of keys to unlock power and authority, to authenticate our most earnest voice. When we realize that even if we have never learned how to stop, to hear, to listen, or how to respond to ourselves, we can learn. We can grow, blossom, bloom, and become. We can start to savor slowing down, beginning to pause, and filling our lungs with luxurious long breaths. We can rest until we hear the earnest call and feel the peace sweep over our being. Bathe us in light. Teach us to receive.

AWAKENING FEELS A LOT LIKE CLARITY, LIKE TRUTH, DOESN'T IT? YOU ARE CLEAR ABOUT WHAT YOU THINK AND WHERE YOU STAND. WHEN YOU HEAR YOURSELF THINK, SPEAK, AND BEGIN TO BEHOLD THE TRUTH, YOU KNOW IT, DON'T YOU? WHEN YOU ARE OPEN TO LIVING THIS TRUTH AT ALL COSTS, YOU FEEL AWAKE, ALERT, AND IMMEASURABLY POWERFUL. FREE.

Even if we have never started a journey into ourselves, we can begin, right? We can, right here and now, can't we? We can start paying attention, waking up to our own voice that has been whispering to us all along. Warning us. Stopping us. Encouraging us. Growing us. Start by taking one tiny step of action in response to the voice inside that never fails or betrays us, never limits or disappoints us. It calls us to arise and move toward freedom. It places keys in our hands, unlocks our life. Do you feel this invitation?

I AM A WOMAN WHO HAS SIGHT OF SEVERAL DOORS THAT WERE UNLOCKED AND OPEN FOR ME, DOORS

POSITIONED AND PRIMED FOR ME TO WALK THROUGH, BUT I WAS BLINDED BY TEARS, COWERING UNDER THE FAUX AUTHORITY OF VOICES OTHER THAN MY OWN, CHASING APPROVAL INSTEAD OF DREAMING DREAMS. ONLY WHEN I STARTED TO HEED THIS VOICE INSIDE OF ME, DID I EVER START TO FEEL HOPE AND JOY. TO DREAM. TO DRAFT AND DETAIL WHAT I HOPED AND CRAVED OUT OF THIS SHORT PUFF OF LIFE WE LIVE. TO PONDER DESTINY.

I share with you the hard-earned answers I found, my friend. I can offer you many keys. May everything I have fought for, dug for, gotten soiled and bloodied for, inspire yours. May these keys unlock the treasure trove inside of you, beloved. May they ignite your keys to victory, peace, and wild personal freedom. May these keys lead you to the ones you carry on the inside of you. May they open the wondrous life you were designed and destined to live. May you be startled awake by the power inside of you.

Practical and Spiritual Steps

1. Where can you create a safe and luxurious space to sit and sink down with your pen and paper and acknowledge the little awakenings that have happened all through your life, day by day? Each day, where can you find a cozy, secluded space and write your remembrances of how life has faithfully awakened you? Has it been through heartbreak? Through grief? Through love or loss? Please silence your phone and your screens, and spend thirty slow minutes thanking your life for how it has awakened you.

2. Dedicate ten minutes to recalling and writing down your last, big, and mighty "aha" moment. What did you discover? What life key did you find?

3. Please write the life you crave to live. Describe the life you yearn for in both broad and detailed words. Write down how your life feels and how you experience and respond to your life. In a reflective and hopeful state of mind, thoughtfully think on your most precious desires. What do they hold?

French Press
~ Moment ~

My friend, I salute you for your doing what many do not do: I salute you for having begun. I lift my mug to you for beginning, for creating the time and space to think about and feel your life. I lift my mug and toast to the person you are becoming and the person you already are.

Now the Lord is that Spirit: and where the spirit of the lord is, there is liberty.

2 CORINTHIANS 3:17 (KJV)

CHAPTER 2

Choosing Freedom

Did you ever read the classic *Peter Pan*? In the very beginning of the book, there is a lovely description of a mom who is waiting for her children to go to sleep, and when they do, she does something endearing. The mom goes over to each child and takes an inventory of all their thoughts. She plucks out the ones that cause angst and discontent and removes the real troublemakers. She visits every child, takes the time to sort out the agreeable from the disagreeable, and relieves each mind.

We crave this too, this clearing, this sorting. Aren't we all in need of this? This wide-open freedom to live in a space beyond the oh-so-many thoughts, assessments, and memories that hold us hostage, disabling us? A place of fresh air, an open field of thought where oxygen is rich and we are not imprisoned by a tyranny of the personal review of our lack, our insufficiencies, where we have failed. The thoughts that chase us into feeling cagey, discouraged, disempowered, and in constant motion, striving for something we cannot name.

For the better part of my life, power meant having the ability to change someone's mind. Power was defined as having the capacity to venture into another's mind and alter their perceptions, attitudes, and mindsets, especially the ones about me. Power held the yearning of the child I had grown up as, desperate to secure the gaze of my father — even if fits, tears, and hostility were the only methods that worked.

We move through our childhood garnering skills, tactics, and blueprints for how life and people work, what makes them tick, respond. There is a breed of difficult people, who do not respond in stable and predictable patterns to who you are. (Unless you count criticism and fault-finding as a type of response or engagement.) And if you have a history of regular entanglements with these difficult folk, you can slowly become depleted of your personal power, your freedom. Like the proverbial frog that is cooked in a pot of warm water as it is incrementally heated up to boiling, not knowing when the heat is too much for it to bear, its movement is paralyzed. Instead of fleeing, it loses its agency and succumbs to the water that kills it.

POWER, OWNERSHIP OVER OUR CHOICES AND THE BEGINNING OF ACTIVELY CHOOSING OUR LEVELS OF ENGAGEMENT IN RELATIONSHIPS, SMACKS OF HOLY FREEDOM TO ME. TO MAKE THOUGHTFUL CHOICES WHERE WE NEED TO, TO EXAMINE WHAT WE DO BY ROTE, OWN WHAT WE DO WELL, AND CHOOSE ADVOCACY FOR OURSELVES: THIS STIRS POWER, AGENCY.

No one tells you how much power you have over your life, do they? Power to choose, to love, the power inherent in prayer and reflection. Power in our habits, in our decisions, in our choices. I grew up feeling an absence of power more than I felt an invitation into personal power. I grew up seeing many relationships as painful tragedies that happened to me, startling forces that took my feet out from under me, buckled me to the ground. I grew up thinking how you manipulate and control someone to get what you want, rather than sharing or asking for what you need. (Unless, of course, anger or betrayal overwhelmed you, and you could only speak the truth of what you needed at the top of your lungs, prostrate on the floor, limbs pounding in futility.)

I couldn't feel my own complicity, my own agreement, to let another tell me who I was and who I was not. My head hung low, awaiting decisions about the fate of my dearest relationships from the verdict of another.

Recently, I spoke with a dear young man in my office, who is almost half my age. He has been on the inside of a relationship that has gone surprisingly south while in the throes of "first love" dating. Subtle and stable cords of manipulation, criticism, and control are pulling strings deep inside of him, turning him into a puppet dancing to try and break free of the mindset of another.

I spent many moments of my week in contemplative thought about him and the difference in our ages, trying to find words for him that I wish had been spoken over me. I wished I had had someone to guide me when I too was in relationships that played upon broken places. I let someone with a whole lot of inner ugly tell me who I was. Listening. Letting it sink down. Taking it in. Then apologizing for my lack.

I came back to the session the next week, wanting to give away what I hadn't been given. Someone who cared to alert me that the patterns we start when we are young follow us, carve out roads for relationships, and become part of how we understand ourselves. I asked him to let my words wash over him, to keep the ones he liked, the ones that worked. But to know, on the other side of twenty years, I wished someone I trusted would have spoken into my life and asked me to think about my choices. Think about my habits, think about what I was calling love. Think about what I considered a loving relationship. Someone to encourage me to define reciprocity and why it's essential for sanity.

"YOU HAVE TREMENDOUS POWER. TRULY A HUGE AMOUNT OF POWER RIGHT NOW, EVEN IF YOU DON'T FEEL IT, OR IT FEELS DORMANT. YOU HAVE POWER IN YOUR ABILITY TO CHOOSE: IS THIS RELATIONSHIP GOING TO HELP ME BECOME THE MAN I WANT TO BE OR WILL THIS RELATIONSHIP UNDERMINE ME AND THE QUALITY OF MY LIFE? CAN WE THINK ABOUT THIS TOGETHER?"

These questions summon our thinking, our engagement, and beckon us to make an assessment, helping us observe ourselves. Our thinking and responding to our lives can be as high as 95 percent unconscious. Ninety-five percent of our decisions, our actions, our behaviors our choices, are unconscious and driven from places deep inside of us that we are not slowing down enough to examine. Five percent of our mind is focused on conscious activity, where we are tracking our grocery list, our need to schedule the dentist appointment, the science project that is due. But above both conscious and unconscious thought is a reflective state of mind, where we sit in a place above our thinking and call on curiosity and reflective thought to understand our lives, our choices. This is the royal stage of thought, where we calmly and thoroughly examine our lives, come to know ourselves, pivot from patterns that break us and burden us. We engage in a higher consciousness of thought.

We can spend a lot of money and time on prayer or meditation retreats, trying to tap into this sphere of calm, this zone of genius where we cultivate "ahas" and disentangle ourselves from the binding grip of robotic, rote, unconscious living. But the truth is, this state of mind is available and accessible through conversations imbued with meaning, insight, and reflection. It is accessible through centering prayer, meditation, journaling, in the return to curiosity about ourselves, our choices. It becomes available to us when we sit in silence, let our inner worlds wash over us, allow the comfort and kindness of God to meet us in our broken and wounded places.

But that kind of personal freedom can be hard to choose when our head is spinning with difficult people and their antics. When a crisis comes and conversations break down, staying in motion and distraction seem to be the only prudent options. In the space of reflective freedom, we can be reminded that we can't and won't change people, even if the change might be best for them, best for us. Freedom reminds us of the choices we feel powerless to make, so we get buried in busy instead. Distracted. Stir our yearnings to disappear into a story, a Netflix series, or a substance that will dull the sharp edges of our lives.

I dried my hair the other morning and began to have a conversation with myself, using the time to talk to myself about what was making a particular person in my life so difficult, so insufferable. I knew it was painful when you can't speak your truth. If you speak it, it will be unheard, dismissed, or twisted. I knew it was painful to stay in silence, when the truth of your experience can be felt in every nerve ending in your body. I knew that it was painful to endure someone's unjust words against you, protect your heart, and not let wrong words control your mood or your day. But I decided that, perhaps, what complicates these matters even more is when you know how injurious a conversation can be, when you know the journey this conversational road will take you, and you use your "freedom" to participate. You choose your engagement, you choose the battle, even if the rules of engagement deplete everything in you. You choose the road because it's reflexive, it's easier, it's known and familiar. You choose it out of habit and out of hope for a happier ending. You get in the car, knowing full well it will crash into a brick wall.

The epiphany comes in our imagination first, traipsing across our mental dashboard, settling into our view. In this place, we can visualize what we need, what we want, the sincere and resolute response of our truest self.

I am a woman who thinks visually, who likes to nail down words with images, concepts with visuals. I am remembering a client who told me of a wondrous resort, centered in the serene space of the big island of Hawaii. Luxury sprawled over acres and acres of property, so vast it has a running tram to take you to the pools, the restaurants, and the lobby, so you stay rested and refreshed. The tram running all hours to shuttle you to and fro. Every morning, my client piled in with her family, on her way to the hotel's spectacular buffet, letting the tram do the driving. All ran well until the tram broke down. The real distance between the amenities was exposed, and the hotel started to feel like a hiking trail. And when it did, more thoughtful decisions came into play, so she would not wear out.

Sometimes we have habits that are often like that tram, where we hop on and into dynamics without thinking where they will take us, how they might break us down. Conversations that we instinctively and intuitively know better to get into, yet here we are again. Aboard this tram, where we lose our ability to steer our own course and destination. Lose our choice and personal volition, because we are operating out of convenience and ease rather than decision and thought.

I AM AWARE OF THE STARK REALITY THAT WE CAN BE BURIED UNDER STORIES, PERCEPTIONS, LIES, THE OPINIONS OF OTHERS, AND NOT EVEN KNOW WE ARE

BURIED. THAT WE CAN BE IN A FORM OF QUICKSAND OF THOUGHTS AND NOT REALIZE WE ARE BEING TAKEN DOWN. WE CAN SPEND OUR LIVES BURIED UNDER SOMEONE ELSE'S WORDS, ASSESSMENTS, JUDGMENTS, AND SPEND OUR ENTIRE LIFE COURSE THERE.

Certainly, we feel the pressure of the neverending tasks, errands, and to-do lists, but never become aware there is a more insidious force at work in our lives: our own propensity to lean into the halting words someone has spoken over us, let someone in their own pain define us, and tell us who we are or who we are not. Madness.

We get closer to freedom when we learn to identify the thoughts we are paralyzed under. When we get clear about whose approbation we are chasing, whose opinion is casting shadows and defeat all over our lives. We get closer to freedom when we honor that there will always be a battle: internal and external naysayers, discouragers, people that might never, ever, like us. But we hold a powerful choice inside of us, where we can hush those voices, still and clarify them; not spending our lives yielding and pandering to the opinions of others at the expense of ourselves. Because we have a key inside our pocket, and we feel it when we operate our day and our lives under the clarity and awareness that we have a choice. We get to choose what we focus on, what we listen to, what we decide to be free of. When we are aware of our power to disallow the wrong people from speaking into our finite lives, manipulating us like marionettes. Start making decisions for our lives and not succumbing to the mercy of another's perception. Take that key out of our pocket and draw a line in the sand. Take action and step onto our own chosen terrain. Breathe in the fresh air of choice.

Freedom swells when we ask the overdue questions: What would our choice feel like? What would not living by our habits and standing in our power look like? When we wonder, who could we become if we set up new rules of engagement, where we took better care of ourselves, our hearts, and our sanity? What would freedom feel like it if we were not driven by compulsions, conversations, or control by another? What if we got to choose, beloved? Where would freedom find us? What if we chose to be more deliberate and selective over who and where we give our power to?

What if we made that choice? What if we put on our high heels, lipstick, and best black dress and stood? Unmoveable. Unshakeable. Fixed and steady in our power. In wild personal freedom.

Are you aware of the power on your life? Do you feel what has been given to you as a gift? Irrevocable. Freely given. Unshakably powerful. This power residing on the inside you. Is it unlocked? Are you a believer in it? Are you sitting in the privilege and the knowing and wonder of this gift given by the hand of God? Are you awakening to this power? Are you open to it? Are you ready to choose freedom by owning more of your life? Is it time? Indeed, beloved, it is!

Practical and Spiritual Steps

1. Grab your journal and tell me, and tell you, where in your life are you desperate for personal freedom? Where do you ache to have more might in your life? Over what area do you yearn to reign? Describe this area in as much detail and description as you can. Grow wild with words and description.

2. Document how freedom and its power dissi-

pate from you. Where are you losing your high heels? Write down where you notice freedom leaking from you. Where is it slipping away from you?

French Press Moment

Oh, my friend, we have come to the best part. This is the time where we remember when and where we are beginning to stand in our power, unmovable. We remember that time when we did not yield out of habit or convenience, but instead, stood on solid ground. We acknowledge that time when we could have bowed down to circumstances or people, but we stood tall instead. We lift our glasses to this treasure of freedom. We bathe in it. We pay tribute to this moment, and we close our eyes and take a sip of this experience, so we can remember how good it feels when we choose to stay in our power, when we choose to stay in freedom.

Cheers!

SHE NEEDS A NEW JOURNAL. THE ONE SHE HAS IS PROBLEMATIC. TO GET TO THE PRESENT, SHE NEEDS TO PAGE THROUGH THE PAST, AND WHEN SHE DOES,

she remembers things,

AND HER NEW JOURNAL ENTRIES, BECOME, FOR THE MOST PART, REACTIONS TO THE DAYS SHE REGRETS, WANTS TO CORRECT, REWRITE.

—DAVE EGGERS

CHAPTER 3

Regret as Revelation

Regret.

THIS IS A MIGHTY WORD THAT ALMOST NO ONE TALKS ABOUT. IT'S A QUIET THIEF, THIS REGRET. REGRET LURKS INTO OUR LIVES, SNEAKS INTO OUR THOUGHTS, RANSACKS OUR MIND. STEALS OUR HOPE. BLINDSIDES US.

This blistering feeling that makes us ache that we didn't make different choices, different decisions.

I have lived a sizeable amount of my life where I did not question my regret; I took the punch of it instead. Let it seize me. Let it confront and torture and incapacitate me. But amen that life grows us, right?

After I took the punch of regret, felt it flatten me out, make its mark, I began to think about it. I began to think about regret, and the power it can hold momentarily, seasonally, or how it can cast a shadow over the entirety of our lives.

I have spent almost twenty years as a counselor, therapist, psychoanalyst, and now as a coach to help people step into the lives they crave to live. I have heard hundreds of stories, sat next to people with hearts full of every shade of regret: infidelity, compulsions, substance abuse, physical and sexual abuse, death of all sorts, and the daily kind of regret that sneaks into our thinking, pelting us with shame and condemnation.

I have heard innumerable stories of the pain that comes when people can't leave their homes, their bed, their cupcakes, or the Coca-Colas alone. The pain that comes when you can't tear down the wall that stretches up between the habit or vice that imprisons you from breaking through to the life you crave. All these regrets coming to our mind, dissolving our ability to generate or create the changes we want, incapacitating us from crying out to God to come and enter these places as cold and as confining as concrete.

HAVE YOU KNOWN ONE OF THESE PLACES OF REGRET?

IS YOUR REGRET SOMETHING DIFFERENT, MY FRIEND?

PERHAPS, YOU HAVE A DIFFERENT STORY.

WE CAN CARRY OCEANS OF REGRETS. THERE IS SO MUCH VARIED LIFE IN THE OCEAN, WE WOULD BE REMISS TO CATCH JUST A FEW FISH AND THINK THAT IS ALL THERE IS. AND THERE IS SO MUCH VARIANCE IN WHAT WE CAN AND DO REGRET IN OUR LIVES, OUR OPTIONS ARE INFINITE. DAZZLING IN NUMBER.

I have spent time fascinated by regret as a teacher, as a helper, and as a friend ever since I had an occasion to know it well, spend a significant period of time with it, let it wash over me so thoroughly that I felt I could finally understand it in language. I finally yielded to what it could teach me about my past, the moment I was in, and the moments I yearned to get to.

Some of our finest teachers arrive on the scene of our lives without us fetching them, don't they?

I never would have sought this kind of teacher.

I never would have looked for this kind of instruction.

I never would have chosen this kind of life lesson unless it caught me.

In the middle of an ordinary, everyday moment, I was about to meet regret in a brand-new way.

I happened upon an Instagram post that was not good for me to see. A torrent of memories washed over me, flooded and flattened me. The chasm between my life and the images I saw undid me to a level I was not prepared for. I was overcome with regret. Memories pointed me to a significant time in my life when I could have made different choices but didn't. A time where I could have said very different things, gone in a different direction, but didn't, because I wasn't thinking clearly or thoughtfully about my choices or how and why I made them.

This occasion on Instagram pointed me to how I could have made more of my time, my life; but I stayed stagnant instead. Refusing growth or change. Wishing in that moment that I could be shuttled back to that place in time, use my voice. Infuse the young woman I was then with the one I have worked hard to become. Tell her to stand taller, speak from her truth, say it kindly and powerfully, but speak.

Just a few images on Instagram, and it was as if I was feeling the same emotions I felt twenty years ago. Like a day hadn't ever passed, let alone thousands of them. Memories can do this, can't they? Keep you out of or move you back to places outside of time. Remind you of all the regret we schlep around, carry around like camels.

I fretted here, in this place of regret. I knew the pattern of grief well enough to try and flee. I have learned that the best way to face an emotion is to let it move through you, breathe into it, let it wash over, and not try to dive under its wave or pretend it is not there. And as I let these waves of regret crash over me, I noticed how much regret looks and feels like grief. And how much I regret of who I was or wasn't twenty years ago has a lot in common with the regret I still feel today.

Still struggling with saying things I shouldn't say and not saying the things I need to say. Still bearing constricting patterns of thought, defaulting into old ways of thinking, hearkening to the ugly inner chatterboxes, raising their voices. And as I started noticing these uglies, I started connecting that the same things I regretted about my life and my decisions are the same things I regret about myself now — if I allow my thinking, my habits, and my words to go unattended.

But as I thought, learned, and prayed, I was stirred toward the many antidotes to regret. I thought about how we might invade our lives with the unleashing of actions and words we *wish* we could have said, or decisions we *wish* we would have made, but in real time. Start to write over our history with new, informed action.

BECAUSE, MY FRIEND, REGRET STICKS WHEN WE FEEL STUCK IN WHO WE USED TO BE. WHEN WE FEEL LIKE WE HAVEN'T GROWN AN INCH, THAT OUR LIVES HAVEN'T MOVED INTO WHERE WE THOUGHT THEY WOULD BE. NOTHING ON THE INSIDE OR OUTSIDE OF OUR LIVES BUDGING. OUR EYES IN THE REVIEW YOU MIRROR, STARING BEHIND INSTEAD OF AHEAD. ASSAILED BY THOUGHTS THAT WE HAVEN'T BECOME WHO WE THOUGHT WE WOULD BE.

These thoughts can be the bars of the caged feeling of regret, bars that make our minds race with

"what ifs," with self-condemnation for who we were, who we often still are.

And as I have been thinking about regret, and how it lands on our lives, thinking about this small word with BIG impact, I have some theories about it. Regret holds the hope of connecting us to grief, to wisdom, to healing action, to the acceptance of the timeless reminder that there are some things we cannot change about ourselves, our lives, our journey. We have made decisions that we can't alter or undo. I get this.

I think it is a reason that we don't always want to slow down and think about our lives. Too much of that pesky regret pushes up to the surface when we think about our journey. What we have missed, who we have been, who we wanted to become and didn't. (Or we have not yet.)

Even now, five young kids are surrounding me. I get up early to beat the crowd, and today I regret not getting up earlier because now they are hungry and want breakfast. I am not done working, but I never regret arriving into moments where I am needed by children who are in the throes of growing and swiftly moving into becoming older kids who will need their mommy less. So, I stop, so this too doesn't become a moment I will regret, a moment where I might respond with irritability rather than responsiveness.

I have flashbacks of regret connected to signature events in my life that I wish I could change absolutely.

- I REGRET THAT I DID NOT SPEAK HEALING WORDS TO MY DEAR FRIEND, WHO COMMITTED SUICIDE THE DAY AFTER WE HAD SPENT THE EVENING FALLING ASLEEP TALKING ON THE PHONE. I REGRET THAT I DID NOT KNOW SUICIDAL SUBTLETIES, THAT I DID NOT COMPREHEND THE HINTS OF DEATH THAT I HEARD FROM MY FRIEND. WE WERE ONLY ELEVEN-YEARS-OLD.

- I REGRET THAT I DID NOT SAY A PROPER GOODBYE TO A MATERNAL FIGURE BEFORE SHE DIED OF CANCER. I REGRET THAT I DID NOT UNDERSTAND THAT EVEN POWERFUL, LEGENDARY PEOPLE DIE OF CANCER.

- I REGRET WHEN THE KINDNESS OF GOD PROMPTED ME TO BUY GROCERIES FOR A YOUNG MAN BEHIND ME IN A GROCERY LINE, AND I DID NOT, BECAUSE OF MY

FEAR THAT HE WOULD THINK I WAS INSULT-
ING HIM, AND I WASN'T WILLING TO TAKE
THE RISK.

- I REGRET WHEN THE KINDNESS OF GOD
  PROMPTED ME TO STOP AND PRAY FOR
  A WOMAN AT A GAS STATION, AND I
  KEPT DRIVING.

- I REGRET THE COUNSELOR I WAS TO SOME
  GROUP-HOME BOYS, WHO NEEDED ME TO
  BE MORE THAN I WAS READY TO BE. I RE-
  GRET THAT I DID NOT GIVE THEM WHAT I
  FEEL THEY DESERVED, THAT I COULDN'T AC-
  CESS SOMEONE BETTER FOR THOSE BOYS,
  BECAUSE I WAS DISTRACTED AND PREOC-
  CUPIED WITH RELATIONSHIPS THAT OVER-
  TOOK MY ABILITY TO SHOW UP PRESENT,
  CENTERED, AND OTHERLY.

But there are patterns of regret that poke at me, pop back into my thinking, reminding me of areas still starving for much growth. These are what I want to share with you, these pesky patterns that undo and unglue even the best of us. Patterns that circle our life keep coming back in a different layer, a different experience of regret. Mine always return me to the reminder of the woman I want to be: awake and alive in my moments, present and available. A woman who has mastered her moods and her temper, a woman who uses her time and life well. My regret always reminds me how I have dropped short in all the above.

I have found that usually if something is true for me, you too might find it in your experience, perhaps different key players or a few degrees in variance. Regret can connect us though, can't it? I have not yet met a person who did not know regret. I have met many who were not inspired to change what they regret, many not driven toward repair or rebuilding, but regret finds us all, doesn't it?

I have studied grief, written about grief, lived through many cycles of it, and I knew that if I were going to move through it well, I would have to face it. All the wretched aspects of it that I would rather not feel. Pay attention to where it was pointing me to review, reassess. I knew that I would have to stand still, learn to breathe through what I would rather push down, deny.

But I also knew, after the pain lessened a bit, that I would need to take an inventory of what it was summoning in me. What did I regret? What would I have done differently? How would I have changed things? How would I have redrafted, rewritten that time in my life?

What did my regret have to teach me?

I got clear about this. Perhaps for the first time in my life, I knew the importance of facing all that I carried, because I wanted to breathe and grow through grief this time. I wanted it to instruct me, shape me, and not just plague and condemn me.

Regret is a state of mind. It is just one place in our wondrous minds that we can access. But when we do access regret, we often access our grief. And grief can be so painful, so consuming and debilitating. It is no wonder why we flee.

When I think long and hard about regret — what it means, what it costs — I start thinking of pain management. I think in terms of how we manage the mental anguish that comes from a past we cannot undo. I think it is revealed to those of us who are not solely interested in acknowledging regret but in moving toward it, leaning into it, so we can rewrite the story desperate for a new ending. I think regret's key has a lot to do with showing up today how we wish we would have arrived in our lives back then. Identifying the thoughts that stalk us. Taking the time to think, to redraft, revise, and rewrite ourselves into the present day, letting our regrets teach us. Take hope and stock in the knowing that we avoid a ton of angst and regret when we do what we ought to do. Show up where we know we are called. Put down our phones and screens, pick up the priority of people. Handle our lives. Turn off our screens, spend our hours and our time well by savoring some slow moments in our lives to get reflective and mindful about our choices and decisions.

CULTIVATE THE DESIRE TO LIVE RESPONSIVE AND NOBLE LIVES. LOVE THE PEOPLE IN OUR PATH. TURN OVER ALL OUR REGRETS TO THE HANDS OF A GOD WHO CAN USE THEM. STOP BEATING OURSELVES UP. CALL OUT FOR HOPE AND A FUTURE THAT IS GOOD.

I so hope this call is for you, beloved. That you are a person willing to pause and think about the regrets that keep finding you, calling you into remorse, harsh words repeated against yourself to resolve it. I hope you will move into the place of regret that feels permanent, irredeemable, and take the time to know and understand it intimately so you can make regret usable, temporary, and redemptive. Stop tormenting yourself about who you are not, and start thinking about who you want to become. Practice becoming her. Rewrite your history with new action, placing brave feet down on new soil. Walk into a future and destiny you would be proud to leave as an example, as a legacy.

Is this you, my friend?

This is an invitation to awaken into a season of life where we halt the anguish of regret and use it as an opportunity to pivot, move into a day that is brand new. May today be a brand-new day for you, beloved. May you feel revelation in you arise.

Practical and Spiritual Steps

1. Letting regret teach us. It does have a lot to teach us, doesn't it, beloved? Can we come into agreement with letting it do so? There is power, absolute raw and earnest power in taking a full inventory of our regrets. Of knowing them and itemizing them, so we can know what we are frittering away our energy with because we are carrying it. Can we do this together right now? Can you say yes?

2. Make a list of the regrets you carry in your mind and heart. Make a full and exhaustive list of all your past regrets. Do not let them overwhelm or scare you; instead, let them serve as good and faithful teachers. What do they have to teach you about how to show up today? How do they inform you to show up as better for tomorrow?

French Press
~ Moment ~

Beloved, are you as grateful as I am that things change and we change alongside them? It is almost as if life grants us the ability to climb up the ladder, ascend to a different place of review and perspective, see who we were, and glance at who we are becoming. I lift my glass to you, my friend, at how far you are climbing. I toast to the person you are becoming, a person bold enough to let regret lead you into a brand-new day. Salut!

Give sorrow words:
THE GRIEF THAT DOES NOT SPEAK KNITS
UP THE OVERWROUGHT HEART AND
bids it break.
—WILLIAM SHAKESPEARE

CHAPTER 4

Honoring Losses

There is a loss that comes when you awaken to the knowing that no one is going to come and make your life better, fix what is broken, or repair what time doesn't heal.

Have you known this kind of loss, beloved? The kind of loss that comes and changes your mind, because it is deep and textured enough to change your heart?

Metanoia. This Greek word bears the profundity of a mind and heart that has been changed, renewed, rebirthed. A mind and heart undone and revamped. Settled. Soothed.

In the Spring of 2015, I was in the middle of this impossibly gorgeous hiking trail, with two wildly beautiful women and all our children. I felt ZERO beauty, only emptiness alternating with pain. I had an inner world lit up with so much angst and frustration that I could not hear laughter, and I could not see delight and joy spread across faces. I was caged inside myself, all hope of moving outside of this dank experience lost, feeling futile, ineffective, at a complete and utter loss.

I don't know where you lose your wonder, beloved, or your sense of beauty, or where you lose your precious mind; but for me, I have lost them all to difficult people that I have tried to love. Instead of seeing the trail and the mountains and the green hills and trees bursting into life, I felt only the girth and the grip of all the hate, the frustration, the rage, and the self-pity that comes when you feel powerless over people and at their mercy for relief. This mindset is so thick and heavy that you cannot see your own free will, your options, the footwork to lead yourself out; so, you stay in sinking sand, stand in precisely the same spot that pulls you down on your face.

Abused.

This place is one step beyond desperate, wide open to the revelation that you are, indeed, powerless over every person you have been in battle with, powerless over every heart you yearn to change, to break open. Powerless over how effectively and efficiently these dynamics keep you locked into patterns that destroy someone more noble and level-headed on the inside. Destroy the inner someone who once felt hope, might, and agency. Possibility.

But on that crisp Spring day, I was awakened by a new breed of loss. As I was diving into description of my latest relational woe, my friends did not know what I was talking about. And as I tried even harder to explain, my friends still had no idea why my distress was so thick and heavy, and I felt impotent in my quest to find words to help them understand. I felt starkly alone in a crowd. Laden with pain I could not solve or express.

Humiliated.

I was utterly pummeled by the awareness of the loss that comes from knowing that no one is coming to fix my life — no superheroes, no capes. Holding this new knowing and the tension that God is indeed omnipotent, omniscient, and sovereign, and still not going to step into these situations and make them all better. This grieving was new and unexpected, this loss of a fantasy that someone was going to come in and rescue me. This loss of the fantasy of someone coming to swoop in and make things well and good, heal my choices, and set up the needed and proper boundaries with people who would not take responsibility for their actions.

I realized that no one I was complaining about and agonizing over was going to change. I realized I was wrecking my life, because of my obsession about making the troublemaking people well. And I was feeling scarily similar to Pig Pen from *Peanuts,* who toted under this dark cloud wherever he went. (His full of dust, mine full of gloom). I recognized that dark cloud could very well become my life song, my legacy, my signature impact on the five girls I am proud to call my daughters. Five precious muses. Waiting on their mom to show them a life well spent. The image of being this gloomy, embittered, resentful cloud, casting shadows on even the finest of hiking trails in early spring, was unbearable.

THE AWARENESS OF WHAT I MIGHT BE IMPARTING TO THEM WOKE ME UP IN A COLD SWEAT LIKE A NIGHTMARE.

Desperate enough to pop the bubble of where my mind lived, tied to undependable people that I was depending on getting better (but wouldn't). Desperate to know and hear the God who came to heal the brokenhearted, while my heart was cracked open enough to hear Him. Desperate enough to try and leave behind old habits that died hard but took me down like quicksand. Habits like complaining, hissing, and fussing (but not doing one darn thing different), head slamming against the same wall.

Sometimes we fall into our pain rather than think through it, don't we? Surrender to the waves of emotion that break us, familiar undertows. Spit out the foam and the sand, the salt water that gags you, because you have been taken down again. And when my communication failed and my tales of woe left my friends confused and unclear, I collapsed into my car and into sobs that rock the body. The kind of sobbing that is guttural and holds the weight of every heartbreak you have known, an amalgam of loss.

Ready to yield to a new and better way of living because you are crystal clear that no one else can make it better.

These battles, hovering over us like Pig Pen's cloud, casting dark shadows over our lives. Some of our battles are mental, some are historical, some are present-day, but a battle is always a battle no matter how it's showing up. Is this not true, beloved?

The toughest battles I have ever fought are the ones that finally taught me that the only way to survive well was to accept what I can change and what I can't and act accordingly. To accept that I could not force change, elicit change, or assume that I was the catalyst for it, I had to look my circumstances in the eyes and make decisions to align myself with truth. I had come to an intersection of choice: I could let my circumstances rule over me, or I could take authority and rule my life from within.

The truth that caught up with me on that hiking trail was that I needed to grow a healthy respect for reality as it was. Inherent in that space of truth was an honoring of reality:

- ACCEPTANCE OF GOODBYES THAT WOULD NEVER BE SAID.

- ACCEPTANCE THAT DIAGNOSES AND DEATH OFTEN COME WAY BEFORE WE ARE PREPARED OR READY.

- ACCEPTANCE THAT WE WILL SUSTAIN INJURIES, INSULTS, AND INJUSTICES THAT WON'T EVER BE MENDED.

- ACCEPTANCE OF PEOPLE WHO WILL NEVER OWN THEIR HARM. NEVER APOLOGIZE. NEVER RECANT.

I think acceptance is flat-out hard. It's painful, it's grief, and it's loss; facing the reality of what is versus what we thought it would be.

When I reflect on that fateful hike, approaching a nervous breakdown in the middle of a nature trail, I realized I was absolutely, positively powerless over everyone else's decisions and choices but my own. If the game were ever going to change, and my life was ever going to get close to good and beautiful, it was going to require me to do some adjusting.

- TO MAKE SOME GOOD CHOICES.

- LET SOME THINGS GO.

- LEARN TO LOVE MY LIFE.

- LET SOME THINGS FALL.

- LEARN TO KNOW WHEN SOMETHING IS MY BURDEN AND PROBLEM TO SOLVE AND WHEN IT IS NOT.

I have come to see acceptance as a place where we can recover hope and a new beginning. A state of mind willing and open to take an honest inventory of our losses, become willing to look each loss in the eyes. Start facing them down rather than freezing or fleeing from their presence. Because, beloved, can't we spend a lot of time battling reality instead of accepting it?

- FIGHTING AGAINST THE REALITY THAT GRAVITY IS OFTEN BOSS OVER OUR BODIES.

- FIGHTING AGAINST THE REALITY THAT KIDS, MARRIAGES, AND FRIENDSHIPS CAN GET UNRULY.

- FIGHTING THE REALITY THAT WE CANNOT MAKE PEOPLE WANT TO GET BETTER, GET SOBER, CHANGE, MEND, OR HEAL THEIR LIVES.

There is hope in our coming into a place of acceptance of the losses that are, as they are.

I think we start getting healed when we start telling the truth about our lives from a place of willingness to have the change begin with us. We become the change we want to see. We accept responsibility for making the choices we need to make for ourselves, no matter what other people are doing or not doing.

I share this journey on the trail with you because one of the greatest awakenings of my life came from the realization that I needed to accept things *as they were* in my life. If my life was ever going to get better, I had to stop pretending magic was coming and going to descend and right so many wrongs. I had to start moving toward putting language toward all I carried for years. I had to turn around and face what I had spent a decent portion of my life fleeing from, too distressing to digest.

Acceptance was the gateway for me to enter into truth, where I would stand and face my relationships, my illusions, my fantasies, and my habits; and slide them all under the light instead of hiding them, pretending, abdicating personal responsibility. Closing my eyes and going to sleep.

I could not keep struggling against the facts of my reality if I wanted to stay sane. I had to start telling the truth, to myself first and then to anyone safe enough to hear me. As long as I was depending on someone else, my circumstances, or other hearts to change, I was at the mercy of a fickle other, and I was losing my own power, my own authority in my life, my own freedom to make choices. Have you been here too, my friend?

I imagine if you have encountered and endured losses of your own. I wonder what road, what trail you were traipsing upon, when the idea of change came to you and overtook you, reformed you, met you with *metanoia*, or made you avoid it. I wonder how and where it became clear for you to begin again, to start honoring your losses. Start crying out for hope and new beginnings, fresh chances and clean slates. Where have you changed your mind because your heart had been changed?

I hold many wishes for you, beloved. I close this chapter with one standing tall in my mind: I wish you the personal power and freedom that comes from acceptance, my beautiful friend, the honor of facing all that your precious life has lost. Perhaps, there might be a part of you railing against me right now. Mentally debating me with arguments on why you cannot accept things as they are, convincing me that circumstances are too dire, too consuming for you to let go and just get back to gazing upon own lovely life.

Perhaps fear, anxiety, and stress have been boss

for quite some time now, making your decisions, dictating your involvement, paralyzing you from accessing your own agency, your freedom. I just ask, "Can we think about this together?" Are we thinking about our choices, our involvement, or have we been trained? Are we accepting responsibility for another's life out of habit? Out of guilt? Out of shame, or out of the implication that we are responsible for another's poor decisions? Can we rethink this together? Can we become more intentional, act with thoughtful self-care? Aren't we worth it? Indeed, we have freedom and destiny awaiting, my friend!

Practical and Spiritual Steps

1. Oh beloved, I am asking us to think about what it would look like if we came to see our reality as it is and honor our losses. I am asking us to see and become aware of our reality and circumstances as they are. Often, this is not an easy task, is it? Cleaning and clearing out the attic can hold more appeal, can't it? But if we started now, staring down our losses together, I ask you: What inner battles could we save ourselves from? What angst? What

grief? What toll?

Where would it be a relief to lift off all our inner torment of feeling, like people who are responsible for it ALL, and hand it over to our God who IS? Can you imagine it? That kind of wild freedom? Can you taste it inside your imagination? Can you envision, turning over these inner hurricanes we carry to God and re-set our inner worlds back to peace? Get refocused on our own lives, even if they are ridden with losses we did not imagine?

One of the heaviest and falsest burdens I have ever known is the feeling that I am responsible for the change of another. The enormous weight of feeling hampered and responsible for another's sobriety, gambling, their physical neglect of themselves. I host war inside me where I am aware of another's capacity to self-destruct, yet there is not an opening, an invitation, or a request for my help, feedback, assistance, or intervention.

Of all things that I have become crystal clear on as a psychoanalyst, it is that people need to ask for help to be willing to receive help. Many times, we are feeling falsely responsible for circumstances and people that no one is inviting us to help with change. We are reflexively reaching in and trying to fix, modify, and control circumstances, because this is the way we manage our anxiety, our distress. We are better off returning to ourselves. We are better off getting clear inside of ourselves, asking the anxiety to whisper to us what it is letting us know and become aware of that. Get clear on what we are feeling, sensing, responding to and why. Get back sanity by asking thoughtful questions regarding what we are needing to accept, what we cannot change. Cry out for courage. Wisdom. A self-owned life.

To be clear, acceptance does not mean approval. It does not mean we approve, condone, support, enable, or foster someone's wrong behavior. It means we keep ourselves safe by not inviting ourselves into circumstances that can hurt us. We think smarter. We become unwilling to turn our inner world into a shaken snow globe because of the decisions and choices others make for their own lives. We stop personalizing and start protecting our peace. Stop muscling our way into another's life choices and start minding our own. Stop focusing on the change of another and start noticing where we, as individuals, are yearning for change and personal freedom.

2. If you scanned your life's losses beloved, where could you give yourself a little more sanity, a little more calm by accepting something or someone difficult, who may very well not change? Is there a person in your life who puts you on pins and needles? Are you hoping they will heal or change? Are you hinged, attached, or overburdened with the change someone else "needs" to make? Is there a circumstance you are not facing that adds weight to your heart, mind, and your life? Can we give it over to your journal as a holding space? Start writing about all you carry. Just pick up your pen and paper and write out your innermost prayers!

French Press
~ Moment ~

We all carry moments we will never forget. Moments that etch themselves in our bone marrow become a rich part of who we are and how we understand ourselves, how we think through and process our lives. When we begin to accept our lives as they are, we are seated in a powerful position for personal change and freedom, even though we may be sitting in a large pool of tears. When we allow acceptance of loss to invade our hearts and thinking, we create a place for possibility for a self-owned, extraordinary life. I lift my French Press to you, beloved, for your thoughtfulness and your endurance. I salute your ability to allow life to craft and cultivate you, chisel you into someone deeper, richer, like the finest of coffees. I send my mug straight to you and with crazy affection say, "You are brave."

YOU CHANGE YOUR LIFE BY

changing

your heart.

—MAX LUCADO

CHAPTER 5

Giving Up Our Grudges

Grudges. They hang on you like a weight. They anchor you below the ground, to the bottom. Tim McGraw has a lyric that says, "Bitterness keeps you from flying." Beloved, do you feel what he is talking about? The kind of inner world toxicity that clouds your ability to see anything beyond the pain you feel? Forget flying; it is enough to just see straight when bitterness invades your body, your heart, and your mind.

These grudges can latch onto us. We can carry them around for years, lifetimes. Their shadows cast a shade of chronic dissatisfaction and discontent, a disabling of our ability to arrive fully engaged into our moments. Sometimes, we can put them down, only to be startled by their return, someone's stinging words throwing us back into the same familiar prison cell. We feel trapped and caged by the emotions we can't get out of our minds, and our bodies alight with rage, sorrow, and white-hot hatred.

Words, injuries, movies, song lyrics — these can put us back into this cage of thought where we hate to be. Where we remember what we yearn to have but can't access what we feel has been taken from us. A place where we are blinded to anything but the ugly we feel. We are breathing in this kind of ugly, a green gas of thought.

Grudges. Drowning inside something we cannot change but feel powerless to accept. Have you been there?

I saw a truck with an advertisement against drowning, and the sign named drowning as the leading cause of accidental death. (Wikipedia said it was the third leading cause, taking 1.7 million lives in 2013.) Drowning can be speedy and silent, and no one can hear you when you are in peril. A little bit of water ingested into the lungs, and breathing shuts down, as do vocal chords. Your life and body are at death's door, and you cannot speak a word. Panic floods your entire being, and you are without language of any kind to bail you out, mute in the face of crisis. Silent in the face of death.

Have you been there, beloved? Drowning in emotions so powerful they feel capable of taking you down, swallowing you on the inside, engulfing you? Gripped by thoughts and emotions so strangling, you lose your voice and your ability to breathe even when you are standing on dry ground? Oh, my friend, I hear you. These grudges, they hold the power to destroy our lives, our joy, and our ability to walk in power, in freedom. Like cold, steel shackles, these grudges can tether us to painful states of mind, their weight making us someone we can't stand to be and feel powerless to change.

A GRUDGE IS A WORD WE FEEL BUT OFTEN DO NOT KNOW HOW TO DEFINE, LANGUAGE DISAPPEARING SOMEWHERE BEYOND REACH. SOMETHING WE CARRY BUT CANNOT COMMUNICATE. A BURDEN WE SHOULDER BUT CANNOT DESCRIBE. GRUDGES TOTING A PSYCHOLOGICAL STATE OF MIND, WHERE WE ARE BEARING A MINDSET THAT THREATENS TO WIPE OUT OUR ABILITY TO STAY PRESENT IN OUR LIFE'S MOMENTS, TO FULLY ARRIVE. A MENTAL BACKGROUND NOISE THAT SABOTAGES OUR ABILITY TO SHOW UP AND ENJOY WHERE WE ARE. OUR JOY

AND PEACE COLLAPSING INSIDE OF US. ELUDING US. GRUDGES TAKE CENTER STAGE.

We are going to nail them down in language, so when a grudge comes and throws us into a pit we do not know how to climb out of, language will become the rungs of the ladder we use to get back to level ground. To be fluent in the language of our inner world is one of the most valuable skills we can ever own, ever master. It allows us to ascend from the circumstances that threaten to bury us and gives us relief. Because nothing can bury us quite as effectively as the slow burn of hateful thoughts that are nursed in the bosom of a grudge. Isn't this true?

A grudge is birthed from the failure of another to own their harm, their violation, the pain they have caused or continue to inflict. A grudge is birthed over wrongs that have not been owned or righted, where accountability never shows up. A grudge is evidence of another's continued failure to acknowledge their transgression, and you are stuck doing the work of reciprocity alone. Grudges come when we feel dependent on people to return what has been taken and fix what has been irreparably broken, focusing our eyes on people and circumstances to generate the repair that does not come.

I have watched and listened to many clients wreck their lives because of their refusal to let go of the grudges they carry, and I have been tempted to wreck my own because of the same thing. I am always tipping my hat to a client I have known for a long time, who has walked through seasons of life in mental and emotional pain that are almost unimaginable. Heinous psychological torment, a robust part of her every day for several solid years.

She was in a marriage fraught with deception, lies, and many, many other women. Evidence would stack, betrayals would mount, and she would be told she was crazy, imagining out of her own insecurities. Exaggerating. Misunderstanding. Failing to trust, the onus was always on her to make straight and understandable what was convoluted and an impossible riddle. Her hate became so thick it became a lens. Her daily grind fraught with rage, sobbing, another lie to untie, another deception to undo. Tormenting, relational equations a constant stream of thought, inescapable and impossible to solve. Blinding.

We can be blinded by hate, can't we? Blinded by rage, by grief, by our own denial, our own refusal to see what is right in front of us. Until one day, all our awareness stacks up, truth starts clicking into place, and our eyes pop open. We recognize things we have known and seen and felt all along. All the riddles we carry fall down like a gentle, tidy row of dominoes, and we are clear.

On an ordinary day, pulling into the driveway of her home, my client awakened to the knowing that none of these lies, deceptions, and betrayals were unclear at all. They all stood tall in neon colors. These uglies and shackles, these years of feeling that messes were co-created realities she was complicit in creating slid off, dissolved.

She had come to the knowing that she was involved, for several years, in unilateral equations she was utterly impotent to solve. She had watched the actions of another for a sighting of repair, took stock in his words, his assessment, believed all he implied, blamed. And in a moment, she felt free because she no longer believed any of it. She wasn't waiting on the truth to arrive, because she was carrying it. She was carrying the whole ring of keys that would allow her to live free.

Sometimes, you have several years of crazy, hard work, unfathomable angst, and one moment startles you into absolute clarity. You are awakened in an instant. You make one of the most significant decisions you can make, because you start to tell yourself the truth. You give yourself permission to acknowledge the degree and severity of all you have endured and suffered, but you get crystal clear of where the repair is not going to come from. You no longer believe the lie.

Sometimes, you become wide awake to the knowing that the person who perpetrated, violated, lied, stole, and/or betrayed you can never bestow what has been taken. This painful truth feels like relief, because you stop hunting it down in someone who cannot give it to you. You stop a fruitless chase, and you step back and start to ask, "How, in the midst of madness and mayhem, am I going to show up and take care of myself in a way I would be proud of? How do I want to live? What do I yearn to have control over? How can I arrive into my life and assume proper responsibility for it? Slip into my high heels, stand with shoulders straight and back, stare down my circumstances, and disable the ability of another to blame me for their failures?"

Wide-eyed and clear that you are not their healer, and repair will not come through you. You were not designed to repair broken men, broken women. You will not stand under the deception and the mindset that all is broken because of you, your lack, your insufficiencies, or where you fall short. All those fingers that have pointed at you, accused you, called you names — you brush away and feel absolved, no blood on your hands. Guiltless.

These trouble-making grudges come like spells, tempting us to fix our eyes on people, transfixed by their every slight and failure. Have you been there, my friend? Are you there now? Do you have a grudge to lift into the mighty hand of God to heal? Do you need help moving hate into something that can be used? Are you sick of self-imploding with issues that you cannot fix? Are you ready to trust in what works: in God, in gratitude, in personal development when your mind is overcome with sludge, the slime of accusing thoughts and falsehoods that have surrounded you?

ARE YOU READY TO FIND STILLNESS AND A WILLINGNESS TO FEEL WHAT WE WOULD RATHER SUPPRESS? LET THESE FEELINGS WASH OVER YOU INSTEAD OF OWNING YOU?

These cleansing waves of grief, relieving us, calling us back to ourselves, summoning truth. Calling us into the grace of God to come and heal and fix what we cannot; to seal our minds from the accusers inside and outside of us. Quieting and stilling us. Setting us free.

Is this you, beloved, who yearns for more abundance? A life beyond what has held you captive? Are you being beckoned into a new chapter of life where the events of old become usable, instructive, and the threshold of change?

Oh, my friend, I have full confidence that this is true. That you are ready and willing and able to step into a brand-new story, where triumph finds you. I tip my hat to you. I stand up and applaud where you are going and your good and noble why. You were born for such a time as this, and I believe this to the marrow of my bones. May you walk into and may you know a brand-new day!

Practical and Spiritual Steps

1. Anne Lamott says something so humorous, that it can make us smile about a painful reality. She says, "Not forgiving is like drinking rat poison and then waiting for the rat to die." Sometimes we are drinking this poison from carrying all these grudges, getting fixated on the rats. Watching these rats hand over our freedom, release us. Is this true? Where is unforgiveness finding us? Where is it trapping us in wrong thoughts about ourselves? Our culpability? Our blame? Where are we tethering ourselves to another, who causes harm? How could we show up in better protection of ourselves? Where do we need to be set free? Isn't it time, my friend?

2. We need to come into agreement about something essential and fundamental. We need to agree that we want to be free, 100 percent free, from people who cause harm and do not own it or apologize. We are not under a spell of an illusion of perfection, but we are thinking thoughtfully about those who do not own their harm. We are becoming aware of patterns of

engagement, where we are left holding the burden, the pain, and the short stick. Where is this sneaking into our lives? This agonizing dance, where we assume responsibility for the vitality and health of relationships that are one-sided, and where harm is invited to come in and ransack us. Where is it finding us? Let's take a few, quiet moments to get clear and thoughtful about where this is showing up. Unlock ourselves from this penitentiary of false thoughts. Choose freedom.

French Press
~ Moment ~

Pain finds us all, beloved, doesn't it? It is our common ground. Uniting us in the knowing that it comes for us all, poking its head up in a myriad of ways. But I lift my mug to you, my friend, because you are on the cusp of moving pain, defeat, and years of toil into something that can be given to another. You are reaching into the enormous pocket of your heart and pulling out compassion and a story to help another in the throes of their pain.

I believe this is one of the kindest gestures we can give one another: finding a story of triumph to meet them in a circumstance that elicits no hope. In this, we begin the process of waking up, becoming aware of ourselves and coming into agreement with who we truly are and how we were meant to live: loved and free. I lift my mug to your story. I salute you in the story that you will tell to help nourish and soothe the broken hearts in your path, who need your voice of victory.

Salut!

Dream no small dreams,

FOR THEY HAVE NO POWER TO MOVE

the hearts
of men.

—JOHANN WOLFGANG VON GOETHE

CHAPTER 6

Wishing Like a Kid

My mom told me I was an old soul, even when I was little. I think this must be true, because I don't ever remember feeling particularly light or dreamy, giggly. I felt burdens and a sense of enslavement to things I "must" carry out, even if that was never the truth. Even if it was just pressure I allowed to bat me around in life, drive me from one task to another, one degree to the next. I did not wish. I did not dream. I yearned to accomplish, instead. Check practical items off my list, catch a rush of endorphins at the end of a meaty list of tasks completed.

But life bottoms out when joy and glee aren't leading, doesn't it? When pressure, circumstances, and drive animate your being, you are at their mercy, you are their pawn, their toy. Under the weight of tension, there is a part of our well-being and sound mind that collapses. Peace and rest elude us. Compulsion finds us instead. Hard, angular thoughts fill our minds, our time; and our watches oppress us, making us feel we are constantly behind, on a treadmill running, huffing, and exhausted but standing in precisely the same spot. Deluged.

Beloved, we can rest and come into peace when we have conversations that need to happen. Conversations that perhaps are long overdue, and yet they arrive in our soul at the right time, salve in the exact place of a wound.

I remember being on the phone with a mentor. I gave my list of all the reasons why life was dissatisfying, and all the people who remained the same. After I ran through my exhaustive list, she asked me to take note of the little wins, the little victories. I started to hunt down the things that were right and good and happening all over my life, but I was not seeing them. As I walked through my days with some slow in my thinking, traipsing my mind with intention of discovering what was indeed working, my heart stretched open. I saw and felt the triumph of little victories of a day when I didn't lose my patience, a moment of work and parenting, smooth and satisfying, a meal plan that worked, a house full of beds that were made and shoes put in ordered rows. As I continued this probe into discovering what was already working in moments and tiny details, I got a distinct whiff of hope.

The hope, my friend, was the awareness that I could expand and puff and inflate what was already working in little ways. I could breathe these embers into something akin to a fire. Noting what is working and creating the space to acknowledge what is right and good, even in a day of shambles, cultivates awareness of the mini-miracles all around us. Opens our eyes wider to take in the bigger ones, and plants the hope of what is possible.

As I tracked what was working in my life and how many difficult and trying circumstances had been eased by my setting an intention, as I noticed the embers of them gather into flame, I exploded on the inside with a surplus of seeds that I wanted to plant in the soil of my life: slower bedtimes, more space in the morning to sit with my God and myself, a math tutor who would take the pressure off my ineffective translations of mathematical concepts. As I started to think about what I wanted and what wishing might look like in real time, my hope started to rise and my thinking soared to a new level of possibility.

I felt like a kid with a new toy: awestruck, smitten, aware of wonder. This was a lesson my best friend Katrina had awakened me to during decades earlier in my life, this capacity to wish things into existence. The glee of casting vision for what was wanted and needed, having it show up and reveal itself. My nose always in a textbook, trying to chase down something more substantial and solid, probably rolling my eyes while she dreamed audibly. Katrina's wishes usually materialized what she needed in the moment and what she yearned for in life: ice-blended mochas, girls' nights ending in Jacuzzi dips and a movie, a prince worth her wait, and delay in finding him.

Wishing didn't become mine until I experienced the joy and freedom that came from moving what you want into words, into language that makes the wish tangible, achievable, possible. When you create the wish and write each inch of it down, your mind moves into what it does best: problem-solving, strategizing, designing and building plans, forging roadmaps, figuring out how to make things possible. Our minds have infinite capacity and capability, sheer marvels each one.

We use our minds for the mundane so often, they grow weary: toting these to-do lists, these worries, these hassles that are thugs of time and mental might. Zapping and draining thieves. Squanderers. We need refreshing. We can be bone tired, exhausted, and overwhelmed, before we have even gotten out of bed. Our days and our lives deplete us, and we ache for satisfying rest, where energy and vigor return and abound. Dreaming and sleep restore the mind, and wishing restores our hope. Wishing rejuvenates us in the places we are parched and pooped and pleading for something a little more life-giving. These pockets of craving, where we feel desperate for more zest. More to this life, which has been leaving us dry, withered, feeling like crumbling leaves.

Can we learn to get wishful? Can we re-learn what, in fact, we may have never learned: this art of wishing? This practice of generating the answers that we have been languishing for? Can we start?

May I ask you, beloved, what you wish for? What you crave? And please tell me, where are you winning, as we speak, as you read? What are your little victories? What are your little wins? Where are your mini-miracles? Where are your big ones? Where has your thinking become so caged that you cannot see possibility anymore? Where does this need to shift? Where can you begin? What area of your life are you feeling a burden to redraft? Rewrite? Remake?

It's time, my friend, to know these good and powerful answers. Let us begin today. Let us begin together.

Practical and Spiritual Steps

1. My bedroom has two French doors that display a tiny garden. For years, I hated the garden it revealed: part vines, part flowers, some wily weeds that kept returning. I would try to work with all the key players, trying to create something cohesive and an arrangement that would welcome the morning and give my eyes a lovely place to land. But after years of dissatisfaction, I ripped everything out and stared at it like a blank canvas. Reimagining it. I started with a clean slate. Sometimes, when we are stuck with an eyesore, a problem that continues to stay knotted, a burden we continue to carry, we need blank space. Sometimes, we need to fetch a blank piece of paper and move the mayhem of our minds onto the page. Brainstorm. Dream again. Crack our hearts open and respond to them by wishing. Give yourself that freedom now, beloved. Move onto that blank page and begin to wish like a kid.

2. Over twenty years ago, I was in a major car accident that left me with a neck and back that can cause me distress and pain. I went to physical therapy and doctors for quite some time

after the accident, and they gave me several exercises I needed to practice daily if I wanted my pain to stay at bay. They are not particularly time-consuming, but sometimes other agendas compete for (and win!) my attention instead, and the pain and discomfort return. I have found that life often works like that too. There are practices of prayer, journaling, acknowledging, and wishing and reimagining my circumstances that I need to do consistently and regularly to manage mental fret and strain. If I am failing, I feel remarkably similar to how I feel if I am failing to do my neck and back exercises: out of alignment, disoriented, and in pain. Beginning with writing exactly where I am at the beginning of each day, one entire page written with a complete list of where I need and yearn to go in my day, is a game-changing discipline. I share this transformational habit with you to encourage you to begin a practice that can and will revamp your day and your life. Check in with yourself, beloved. What do you wish for? Where does your life beckon you to bring in fresh air and turn you to practices that work? Where is your journal? Can you begin, right now, to answer these questions, and indeed, can you begin to wish like a kid?

French Press
~ Moment ~

One of the first wishes I remember making as a grown woman and a homeschooling mom was for a math tutor to come and break down mathematical concepts into language that my girls would come to own and love. The wish felt enormous at the time. Like wishing for something that was impossible, like being able to give my daughters a flesh and blood unicorn, though my heart swooned at the idea.

I am delighted to share that the wish came true. For three years, I have been proud to have a math tutor come to my girls and teach them in a delightful way I never could. The wish that felt akin to the impossible has become a reality for three, solid years. But it started with an articulated, audible wish. A moving of desire into words, into language and speaking that hope over my life.

What calls and beckons us is wildly and gloriously different, and sometimes it might be uncannily similar. But I lift my glass to you, my friend, and toast to you embarking on a journey toward what you wish for. What you wish for today and what you wish for your life. I lift my mug and toast to the wonder your life contains. I wish for you to knock out everything on your wish list. I salute your desire to begin and return to the practice of wishing like a kid!

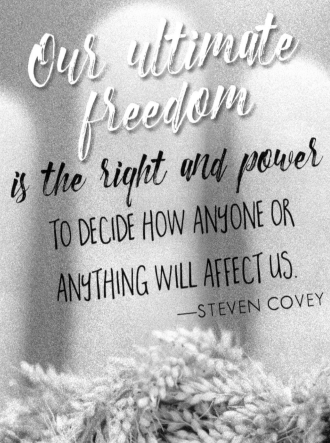

Our ultimate freedom is the right and power to decide how anyone or anything will affect us.

—STEVEN COVEY

CHAPTER 7

The Power of our Peeps

I have a question. I am dying to see if you agree with me. Would you agree that people are just about as contagious as a common cold or the flu?

Do you agree that people can be, and often are, as powerful as any strain or virus that is going around? Beloved, are you paying attention to how the company you keep affects you? Are you tracking how others make you feel? Are you wide-eyed and aware of the powerful impact the people in your life are making on you?

Certainly, there are people in my life who can make me feel like I have been hit by a semi-truck after I depart from them. Like I've been run over and flattened and squashed into the ground, dirt and filth all over me. Do you have these people too, my friend?

I don't know if your house has quite the same degree of messes that mine does with having five kids, but not only do we have two vacuums in the house; in the garage, we keep a Shop-Vac. Because there are always spills, accidents of all kinds, broken glass, liquids, you name it, we have the Shop-Vac to suck up our most trouble-making mishaps. The Shop-Vac is powerful and mighty. It gets the job done, but I have also noticed that there are people like our Shop-Vac. People who come into our days and suck the joy and glee and hope right out of it. Shop-Vac any good we feel, any optimism. Can you relate to this kind of experience, of being Shop-Vacced by a person?

Do you have someone like this?

Do you have someone in your life who hurts you, beloved?

I do too.

I have someone in my family who, out of their own pain, can cause me great pain. My heart, my mind, and my life can ache because of their words, their failure to see me for who I am, accept me as I am. A phone call, a text, an occasional dinner, and I can have fresh thoughts about grudges, can start to feel like these injuries have never left me.

But this is what I have come to remember and what I continue to counsel myself with:

I MUST KNOW MY GOD-GIVEN WORTH. BECAUSE

THERE IS A NATURAL TEMPTATION TO BEGIN TO SEE OURSELVES THROUGH THE SAME CRITICAL LENS AS A HURTFUL OTHER, TO SEE OURSELVES THROUGH THE SAME HARSH EYES AND BEGIN TO DEVALUE OURSELVES. THERE IS A PROFOUND TEMPTATION TO BE PULLED INTO THE PERCEPTION OF ANOTHER'S FIXED MINDSET AND LOSE OUR FEET RIGHT OUT FROM UNDER US. THERE IS A BETTER WAY.

We must awaken to the knowledge that we not only keep company face-to-face, sometimes by the assistance of technology, but we keep company with people in our minds, hearts, and in our thoughts. We can generate our own thoughts or default to the words others have spoken over us. We can meditate and chew and ingest the thoughts of others, swallow them whole. Allow them to influence and persuade us. Nourish or poison us. Determine our day and the quality and vitality of our lives.

Have you ever caught yourself in the middle of an intense dialogue or confrontation occurring in the secluded place of your mind? Have you heard yourself repeating points of clarity, of fact or feeling, yet only in the silent arena of your thinking? Oh, my friend, I have too, many times! I am in a constant holding room, hosting conversations in the confines of my mind. Carrying people and dialogues as I fold laundry, sweep the house, decide how to respond to a surly comment.

It is here, in the privacy of our own minds, we must discipline ourselves to consciously choose and rethink the thoughts and people who can influence and control our thought life. Make a resolute decision as to who we allow access to our most private and prized places. Become extraordinarily selective with which people are given a key to the sanctuary of our souls.

Earl Nightengale nailed truth when he said,

"WE BECOME WHAT WE THINK ABOUT."

IF WE BORROW HIS WISDOM, HE UNVEILS A POWERFUL AND PROACTIVE WAY TO BEGIN TO PAY ABSOLUTE AND DETAILED ATTENTION TO WHAT (AND WHO) WE ARE THINKING ABOUT.

To begin a conversation inside ourselves and learn to think through our relationships with people and their words. To begin to ask and question, "Whose thoughts are we thinking, and are these thoughts servicing us, or are they a disservice? Are they helping us or hindering us? Are they creating hope or carrying harm?"

I cannot get an example out of my mind. I remember being in a familiar and repetitive agony over trying to change someone's mind, because their path and choices were causing me a tremendous amount of distress and anxiety. I picked up the phone, because I did not know how to solve this kind of mental and emotional strain inside my own thinking. In this moment, I felt invisible, irrelevant, unheard, and dismissed; and all felt true of me in that space of time. The weight of all these shades of despair was collapsing my ability to think through, make sense of, or process anything else.

I got on the phone with someone I knew, who had all these similar feelings under her belt, knew these darker shades, and had the skill to help me navigate through them. Without missing a beat, my mentor told me to change the story of the narrative I was suffering under. To write a new story of the person's decision that did not have me inside of it. She told me to settle down, to sit and imagine how this story, this scenario, had nothing to do with me at all. She told me to pick up a pencil and legal size piece of paper and draft a story of that person's decision-making that did not include me in it.

I wrote the story with a pencil gripped violently in my hand, my fingers white and sweaty from the pressure, the pencil cracking. I wrote until I was clear. I wrote for as long as it took to get outside of myself and into the royal road of thought, where I was aware and confident that I am not responsible for the decisions made by grown adults. I wrote until I was clear that the decisions made from another are not my burden, my life call to change. I wrote until I was calm and was perched in a higher place outside of my own thinking, where I could look down at myself and feel compassion, love, and absolutely absolved. I wrote until I felt free.

My mentor encouraged me to write as a means of harnessing and choosing detachment, to consciously and deliberately choose a different state of mind that did not have the same personal story of injury inside it. Tell a new story without a wounded and wronged me in the center of it. One that didn't personalize the slight, their failure to listen to my words, my pleas. She asked me to write a narrative, a story where I could be free of blame, free of self-condemnation. Write myself out of this story of heartbreak and the tyranny of a painful person. To ask, how would I then live if I knew their story had nothing to do with me?

In this sea of life, there are people who can mentally drown us. When we hold on to a personalized account of the "drowners" and their dunking actions, hold fast their thoughts and choices, hold tight to our reactivity, our bitterness, our grudges; it's like clutching onto an anchor and sinking to the bottom of ourselves, of our lives. Can you feel this? Can you find this experience inside you? This unbearably weighty anchor of thoughts and feelings that can drown us, pull us under water. Stop us from breathing. From thinking.

Beloved, there is a life raft of perspective, of holding onto our worth, of depersonalizing the hurtful arrows inside another's words and actions. When we don't let their failures, their harm, control our lives or our hearts, we stay afloat. We keep from going under the waves that can knock us out, drain and drown us.

Our energy is finite, isn't it? Nothing can drain our energy more effectively than the difficult people in our lives. Nothing can rob us of energy more effectively than nursing our grudges, our injuries, and the insults we carry records of. These grudges and heartbreak, my friend, are often our common ground. We can relate to each other here, can't we?

In these moments, when we are adrift in the middle of the ocean and feel like we are drowning, we need to learn to think deliberately, to respond instead of reacting. We must remind ourselves that this life is short, that we are seated in a powerful position of steering our course, sitting at the helm of many of our thoughts. We can awaken to knowing that clutching our even rightful grudges will never make us better; they will only make us bitter. That even with our most signature wounds, we must rethink and move toward a different beginning. Not because we have forgotten or because we have excused them or grown weak, but because we crave something beyond them.

WE MUST ALLOW OTHERS THEIR OWN EXPERIENCE, SO WE CAN BE SET FREE. WE GIVE UP OUR GRUDGES AND OUR WOUNDS AND PLACE THEM INTO THE HANDS OF GOD, SO WE CAN BE FREE.

We hand over the difficult people in our lives to the only person powerful enough to handle them: them and their God. We give them over, so their weight is not on our shoulders but in the hands of a God who can change hearts, remove burdens, and set us free.

Although there are many destructive people in our lives, who can invade it and rob us, there are also opposites. There are also people who make us better, stronger, braver, and more hopeful than we could ever be without them. There are people who speak life and kindness and encouragement, who save us from the loneliness and discouragement we feel is stalking us. There are people who keep us afloat.

Sometimes our lives are lit up with people who are indeed light-bearers. People who light up our lives with encouragement and counsel, nourishing meals and conversations, hope. In their presence, we are crystal clear that there is probably no greater gift this side of eternity than the power of people and relationships to create and sustain beauty in our lives. Seek them out.

Sometimes, we must move out of our comfort zones to seek and find the people we need. We need to fetch the kinds of relationships that will speak into our parched places, into our hunger. Sometimes the onus is on us to find and fill our lives with the relationships we need. Find them in groups, find them in church, find them on the inside of books. They are there, waiting for us. Speaking our language.

I have heard a lot of aches in my practice. A myriad of regrets, failures, hauntings, poor decisions. I have heard of the pain that comes from sorrow, the pain that comes from grief and loss. Yet, I don't know if I have ever heard cries like those from people who yearn for friendships they don't have. The grief that comes from loneliness, from feeling entirely alone in a world abounding with people, the utter emptiness of technology to satisfy.

In the throes of a culture of Facebook "friends" and followers, our hunger for what is real and trustworthy does not change, does it? The fleeting satisfaction of "likes" and "loves" is stunningly hollow when we were designed for much more. We were designed to be knit inside a tribe and community to shield us from the storms of life that can encase us. We were designed to be sheltered and protected from the elements of life, to enjoy authentic friendship and connection with people who have our best interests tucked in their hearts and often are the means through which we can endure this life. If you don't have them, beloved, isn't it time to find them?

I ASK YOU, MY FRIEND, WHO ARE YOUR PEEPS? WHO IS IN YOUR CORNER AS A VOICE OF ENCOURAGEMENT AND LIFE? WHO SPEAKS HOPE OVER YOU?

Who in your life maxes you out or Shop-Vacs you, runs you over with agendas or criticism? Where are you getting knocked out instead of built up? Where might your tribe be established around you? Where could you use more of a buffer against the elements of life? Where could you use more protection? Where are you most vulnerable, and who is most protective?

Determining our peeps is one of the most powerful things we can do. The people we surround ourselves with build our lives or tear them down. This is the time to create the life we have craved by taking thoughtful inventory of our peeps. In this way, we are proactively planning our future. We are building it for a better, brighter day. We are ready to do this!

Practical and Spiritual Steps

1. Let's know this well, beloved. Who controls much of your mind and life right now? Is this person known to you instantly? Is this person good news? Where might you better protect yourself from harm?

2. Make a detailed list of how many people you know, who actively build up you and your life? Next to your list, how many people do you notice, who regularly tear your life down? How could you manage your life to make sure you have regular and dependable contact with more builders than destroyers? Are there any "optional" destroyers that you could have less interaction with?

3. Take a moment and envision yourself as the captain of your ship. I want you to fill up your boat with the people you most want aboard. Who is getting on your boat? Are the people on your boat friends and family and those familiar to you, or are they people you yearn to meet or know? I want you to fill your boat with people who will make your trip lovely and enjoyable.

People who will surround and empower you to not only stay afloat but enjoy the ride.

French Press
~ Moment ~

Celebrate a person, a friendship, a connection that is of high value to you. Take the time to arrange a lunch, dinner, or a conference with someone you know will add tremendous value and vibrance to your life. What can you toast to, cheer, and celebrate? What are you grateful for in this moment? Where are you eager to lift your mug of coffee, tea, or lemon water to celebrate and savor? And with whom?

You were born for such a time as this.

CHAPTER 8

Overcoming Ordinary

I have held a life story of anxious and fearful thinking, beloved. I have known the many pesky and persistent kinds of fears — heights, public speaking, how I seem to daily fail my children in important ways — that can cause my cheeks to flush red with regret and remorse.

I have lived in a mind sealed with bondages, invisible bars that kept me caged, constrained, controlled, and commanded by fears. I remember panic attacks so frightful in elementary school, they would rob me of my voice, my words a stream of stutter and halted language, nonsensical. I can locate myself in my 4th-grade classroom, where we traded turns reading *Island of the Blue Dolphins*, and see myself standing front and center of the classroom reciting U.S. states and capitals. I stood on legs that shook, exposed earnest fear, and taught me that our bodies reveal what we hold. Not faking it the way we can, our bodies tell our secrets, all we grin and bear.

A gigantic and novel fear emerged. It found me after forty years of age, while perched in front of a streamed movie on my sofa, my kids piled up all around. After five labors, seventeen different homes, losses and heartbreaks of every kind, a signature fear emerged: What if I am average at everything I have ever done — average in who I am, average in any way that is measurable, average in any way that counts? What if average is all I have ever been and all I will ever be?

Fears bring along a loathsome tribe of cohorts, don't they?

A fear of being average can fetch trepidation, render us feeling disqualified, benched, and sidelined in our own lives. Disqualified from running in the races we were meant to run. Setting up a lens of opposition: us versus them. Most of my life, I have felt disqualified from something I wanted because of who I was or wasn't, too much or too little of something needed and essential. My background, my past, my lackluster 2.0 high school GPA, my familial and parental failures — all falling short of the perfection I tied to those seemingly qualified to use their voice, speaking into the lives of others in a public space, calling them to action.

ALTHOUGH I NEVER FELT QUALIFIED TO SPEAK IN PUBLIC, I WOULD OFTEN DRINK IN THE MESSAGES OF THOSE WHO DID. THOSE BRAVE ENOUGH TO SHARE THEIR STORIES, WHAT THEY HAD LEARNED ON BEHALF OF US ALL, CALLING US TO HIGHER GROUND. BY PROFESSION, BY HOBBY, BECAUSE IT IS MY JOY AND DELIGHT TO CATCH THE PULSE OF SOMEONE'S LIFE SONG, I LISTEN.

One day, and then several days back to back, I listened to podcasts by a mother of many, who lives a lovely and heartfelt life as she pursues teaching the love of literature with her tribe. Authentically and publically, she inspires this love of reading, and I am taken to the ground with envy. Envy of how she has what I could only hope for: the courage to use her voice. I am awash with gratitude for her and also holding profound and painful envy of her, because she seems to be living the life I missed.

I create imaginary stories of her out of this envious place. Spin tales of how she meets all the criteria for an above average, qualified life. My mind drumming up all the reasons why she has it all together, and I sit suffering. I am busy stringing mental stories together of how her life landed so perfectly, enabling her to do what she does so well. I sit spellbound by the beauty of who she is, stuck in my thoughts of my own average, disqualified thinking. Months pass, and I feel the noose of comparison and the bondage of self-preoccupation. The confinement that comes when you pit your life against someone you do not even (fully) know. Let loose this thug and thief of life: comparison. Let it steal every shred of peace of mind, every ounce of sanity. Stack yourself against someone you don't even know. Madness.

GOD CAN USE EVERYTHING, CAN'T HE? EVEN ENVY, THIS TERRIBLE GREEN GAS OF AN EMOTION, POLLUTING OUR MINDS AND HEARTS, PUTTING POISON IN OUR WORDS.

I did have a past with envy. I had written my doctoral dissertation on it. Knew how to recognize its stirrings, causing us to say discounting, hurtful things because we are trying to manage our pain. Envy can turn us into slanderers and people who discount the good that others are doing. Fetch out the ugly in beautiful people doing noble and courageous work. Wretched: this envy.

But beloved, envy can also point and pivot us, its embers alighting our bellies with fire. Kindling reminders of a life we are drawn toward. Envy can cause us to think and to imagine, a compass for direction if we use it well. Here, I started to dream out of contrast. Contrast for what I wished for my life: full blown freedom to use my voice, to lift faces and call women into the lives I know they were divinely destined to live and in which to find the deepest fulfillment.

I had a moment of awakening while walking my dog around the block: All the imperfect have a call. All are created to live a life using their gifts, to bestow them and live generous and productive lives. Calls that bring us into wrangling fears to the ground also have us turn around and face the fears we may have spent our entire lives fleeing from.

Sometimes, this facing of fears causes us to march straight into our illusions, our constructions of the "perfection" of others, the spell and stranglehold of these binding thoughts. I began with these truths standing tall, absolutely clear that I was not perfect, my marriage wasn't perfect, and my parenting was so far from perfect. Then it finally occurred to me that I have needed and have been fed by humility and humanity far more than I have ever been fed by perfection, and I wondered if it was true for others as well. I realized that I had a choice available to me: I could spend my life pursuing myths of perfection and creating formulas on how perfect people became that way; I could chase authorization and approval from people who may, in fact, be unable to give it to me; or I could pursue the dreams God had tucked in my heart. Arise, and let Him clip the chains and shackles to set me free.

IN THIS LIFE, I AM TAKING A LEAP OF FAITH INTO A PLACE I BANISHED MYSELF FROM DREAMING ABOUT, BECAUSE I HAD IMAGINED IT RED-TAPED AND BANNED FROM ORDINARY WOMEN. BUT WHEN I PEEKED AT MY LIFE, KISSED FIVE CHILDREN GOODNIGHT, AND SPENT MANY MOMENTS AND DAYS WITH PEOPLE I SHARE LIFE WITH, I REALIZED THERE WERE NO ORDINARY PEOPLE, ALL AROUND ME ARE MARVELS.

When I observed the many "ordinary" people in my life, it awakened me to knowing that not one was, in fact, ordinary. The truth was, they were all extraordinary. That day, the illusion of ordinary broke. If I am willing to look at my five girls and know that not one of them is ordinary, I have to extend the same logic to myself and know I am not ordinary either — and neither are you, beloved.

I end this as I am looking at my bookshelf, brimming over with authors and thinkers of every sort. All put on their brave to do so. They stopped listening to the inner and outer critics of their lives, spoke their vision, their heart. I am so grateful that Roald Dahl didn't compare himself to C.S. Lewis and Maya Angelou wasn't halted by Harper Lee. E.E. Cummings kept composing poetry in the shadow of the legendary William Shakespeare. Each one could have trembled at the thought they were just ordinary, nothing original, nothing worth printing by a publisher. I am awakened by this bookshelf as a reminder that we must chase our gifts and go where we are called.

Ethel Waters reminds us: "God don't make no junk." He doesn't make ordinary or average; He makes us all signature, stand-alone creations and gives us a bounty of dreams and visions to walk in. Is this your experience, beloved? What stirrings beckon you? What life would you live if you challenged every thought that stopped and hindered you — pelting those thoughts with good questions? Interrogating every hindrance? Who and where could you be, beloved?

Can we go there, beloved? Isn't it time? You were born for such a time as this.

Practical and Spiritual Steps

1. Have you too been stalked by the thoughts of being average? Felt like you were sidelined and benched from life because you were too ordinary to contribute or play? Have you known the tendency to compare yourself with others in your imagination? Granting the storyline of their lives with all the endowments you feel your life doesn't have? This slope is slippery, isn't it? Reflexive almost. Exposed, we have lived under mindsets that are constructed out of illusions and unquestioned untruths, assaulting ourselves through comparison and contrast, through imaginations of someone else living what we yearn to live. Painful and

excruciating madness.

What if we changed the game right here, be-loved? Took ourselves to a peaceful place, where we could sink into our minds, free of thoughts of comparison or contrast? Hush the voices whispering "average" or "less than"? What if, in-stead, we let our imaginations go wild with stir-rings from this tranquil space? What would we yearn to do from this place? What if we had no inner or external limitation or opposition but were, indeed, free to wish and dream and rec-reate and enter life with our signature? What would life look and feel like? Who would we be? What would we reach for? How would we serve and show up? Where would we soar if we took down these shrinking thoughts of average or less than average? Where would we go?

2. Extraordinary is possible. There is a slower, more earnest and thoughtful place inside us that teaches us the path of extraordinary. There is bounty and abundance in silence, in feeling ourselves, our inner world, and all that we out-pace and outrun. There is a rush of energy that comes when we sit in thoughtful inventory of the good and lovely all around, rinsing our

minds of the mundane by witnessing how and where the extraordinary and tiny miracles are showing up and changing our day.

I took an evening flight home two days ago, flew into John Wayne airport at 9:38 p.m., peeked out my airplane window at the Orange County area lit up below like an extravagant piece of jewelry. Even the notorious freeways, replete with tens of thousands of moving cars, looked like flowing ribbons of lights. All that looks condensed and compacted on the ground looked sparkly and invitational from a higher perspective — when time slowed down and I took the time to notice what was good and lovely.

When I paused and felt the invitation to see my "ordinary" stomping grounds from an elevated and more serene vantage point, I begin to wonder at the city where I live and move and often don't even see because of the hustle and speed of daily life, missing the extraordinary all around. Can speed and busy and worry and stress and old stale stories invade your mind too, stopping you from missing the extraordinary moments sprinkled over your day, like the light you can see on a night flight? Could you quiet yourself and ask yourself: Where is beauty showing up in my "ordinary" and "average" day? Begin to ask: Where do I need to regularly peek over my life and see the good and lovely? Where do I need to savor some slow and start to listen by turning inward? Start to notice the beauty surrounding you. Invite the still, small voice to whisper the hope you were created for. Because, beloved, you were created for a time such as this!

French Press
~ Moment ~

How loudly can I lift a mug of coffee and tap it into yours to tell you how honored I am to have taken this journey with you? I lift my French Press coffee to you, filled with the finest Lost Bean coffee beans, and salute you for the journey we have shared. You are brave, beloved. You are a wonder, a marvel, a gift of a person, and I am ever grateful for having shared this journey with you. Salut! One thousand cheers, and again, Salut!

Arise, Beloved:

AN AFTERWORD

> ## I have looked over and seen the promised land.

—MARTIN LUTHER KING JR.

No one tells you how good it feels when you decide to own your life. No one tells you how freeing it is when you begin to stop making excuses, take responsibility, make better choices, and commit to ways that work.

I have stumbled and staggered and lost sight of this truth most of my life, because I sought approval and authorization from people who could not give me either. I sought to change people who would not change, sought to be seen and understood by people who did not have the eyes or ears to do so. I have spent the better part of life chasing down imaginations of what my life would look like with more degrees, the approval of more people, how I would look and feel if I were ten pounds lighter and jeans slipped on without wrangling or struggle.

I have sat under the spell of illusions and fantasies that someone else could hand me the life I yearned for, lop off parts of me that slowed down or halted my access, and have them criticize and critique me into who I wanted to become.

Beloved, we carry patterns and wrong mindsets that control our lives, don't we? Hold thoughts that undergird every aspect of our being. Our very own minds serve up thoughts and imaginations that block us, strangling life and hope. An enemy's finest work is inside our minds, our habit of coming into agreement with false but powerful tales, lies. Loud, clamoring, and unchanging stories magnify our lack and insufficiencies, returning us to the woe wrapped around our lives. All these thoughts block us from seeing the mighty hand of God ceaselessly working in our lives, using all our ugly for His purpose of good. Chiseling us. Nudging us awake to use what we loathe and detest for wild growth, personal change, and freedom.

I have been a woman held captive in her own mind for decades, but in several pivotal places, change and nourishing thoughts and questions found me. I would be on a walk, a hike, or a stroll down the block, and I would come back home a different woman, because I was led to question the validity of the accusations that I had been disqualified, a woman eternally benched from speaking hope because of who I was and failed to be. I started questioning, "What if who I have been is less important than who I could become? What if God is bigger and grander than all these obstacles that have held me prisoner as long as my memory stretches back? What if these obstacles are opportunities for me to flourish on the other side, if I press in and see them through?"

Beloved, sometimes we lock our gaze on our problems, our history, and our struggles, rather than on a God who inspires us to overcome our problems, bury our shame under our feet, and make us stand taller and with more heart than we would have ever had without them.

On these morning and afternoon strolls, I started to cross-examine my own mind. I saw its fixation and rote habit of repeating old and dated stories that were straight-up desperate for a new ending. As I got stronger and more disciplined and awake, I started to challenge these stories, put them in a witness seat, and question their authority, their endings, their right to have access over the entire course of my God-breathed life.

We can derail our own lives out of habit. We can host thoughts in our minds that assuredly and absolutely undermine the entirety of our lives. And, we may never even stop to question this propensity to live under wrong thoughts and false accusations. Our bad habits of thought and fixed mindsets can pull us into a pit of despair and guilt so thick and deep that we stop looking for ladders to help us climb out. We can get accustomed to and complacent about living flat-out depressed, dismal, and defeated lives, never even questioning if there is another way. We can stop wondering if there is hope, if there is a path out and up, or if change is earnestly possible. Sometimes we set our gaze to qualify, absolve, and rescue us; rather than partnering in willingness and wisdom with a God who is eternal and transcends all.

So, I ask you: Are you ready to awaken to wonder? Ready to begin seeing yourself as a marvel, divinely designed for a destiny only you can carry out? Are you ready to claim your personal agency and freedom? Are you ready to look at your life and see something fresh and lovely coming right around the corner?

This is true: We have all been created for something extraordinary, which would blow the circuitry of our minds if we knew the height and width and depth of our destiny. We know this in our bellies, don't we?

Beloved, this book is a love letter and an invitation into the life you were hand-picked to live. May you feel the peace and joy and everflowing goodness of a God who calls you into a life wider, deeper, and higher than any dream you could imagine. May the Spirit of wisdom and revelation open your eyes and heart and mind to a brand-new day. May you dash right into this abundant life unabashed and unafraid. May you share in the bounty He has prepared for you. May you call on His good name.

I Do Not Like Goodbyes

I am a woman who has dodged saying "goodbye" most of my life. Goodbyes always felt painful, premature, and permanent; so, I slid out of saying them at all. Sometimes, I wish deeply that I would have said them, found words to speak all I carried to the person I was saying goodbye to. Harness the language to let the person know how they impacted me and why. Buckled down and disciplined myself to let people I love become aware of their signature influence on me. Popped the bubble of denial that assured me that there would be another time or occasion to say the goodbye that needed to be said.

BUT, WE CAN GROW THROUGH WHO WE HAVE BEEN, CAN'T WE?

Become people who profit from their past? Move into better futures, because our eyes are open wider and our hearts more alert to who we want to become.

I delight in knowing that, in this new time of technology and global connection, often we do not have to say goodbye. Our journey can continue and deepen. We can take journeys together that do not end. Keep traveling and exploring alongside each other. Climb the rugged terrain of the mountains in our lives; strengthen, and experience them under our feet.

If this journey is for you, my friend, please find me at CCEvansPuglise.com and allow me to invite you into the next chapter. It is going to be good, beloved.

CPSIA information can be obtained
at www.ICGtesting.com
Printed in the USA
FSHW02n1430140618
49166FS